Reading and Writing
In Freshman English I

First Edition

Michael Wilson, editor

Watersgreen House

© 2014 Michael Wilson

Watersgreen House

ISBN-13: 978-0692296318 (Watersgreen House)
ISBN-10: 069229631X

Visit us at http://watergreen.wix.com/watersgreenhouse

or https://www.facebook.com/watersgreenhousebooks

Cover art: *Autumn Landscape with Fox*, Bruno Liljefors (Sweden)

MANUFACTURED IN THE UNITED STATES OF AMERICA

Contents

The Tell-Tale Heart
Edgar Allan Poe

TRUE!—nervous—very, very dreadfully nervous I had been and am; but why will you say that I am mad? The disease had sharpened my senses—not destroyed—not dulled them. Above all was the sense of hearing acute. I heard all things in the heaven and in the earth. I heard many things in hell. How, then, am I mad? Hearken! and observe how healthily—how calmly I can tell you the whole story.

It is impossible to say how first the idea entered my brain; but once conceived, it haunted me day and night. Object there was none. Passion there was none. I loved the old man. He had never wronged me. He had never given me insult. For his gold I had no desire. I think it was his eye! yes, it was this! He had the eye of a vulture—a pale blue eye, with a film over it. Whenever it fell upon me, my blood ran cold; and so by degrees—very gradually—I made up my mind to take the life of the old man, and thus rid myself of the eye forever.

Now this is the point. You fancy me mad. Madmen know nothing. But you should have seen me. You should have seen how wisely I proceeded—with what caution—with what foresight—with what dissimulation I went to work! I was never kinder to the old man than during the whole week before I killed him. And every night, about midnight, I turned the latch of his door and opened it—oh so gently! And then, when I had made an opening sufficient for my head, I put in a dark lantern, all closed, closed, that no light shone out, and then I thrust in my head. Oh, you would have laughed to see how cunningly I thrust it in! I moved it slowly—very, very slowly, so that I might not disturb the old man's sleep. It took me an hour to place my whole head within the opening so far that I could see him as he lay upon his bed. Ha! would a madman have been so wise as this? And then, when my head was well in the room, I undid the lantern cautiously—oh, so cautiously—cautiously (for the hinges creaked)—I undid it just so much that a single thin ray fell upon the vulture eye. And this I did for seven long nights—every night just at midnight—but I found the eye always closed; and so it was impossible to do the work; for it was not the old man who vexed me, but his Evil Eye. And every morning, when the day broke, I went boldly into the chamber, and spoke courageously to him, calling him by name in a hearty tone, and inquiring how he has passed the night. So you see he would have been a very profound old man, indeed, to suspect that every night, just at twelve, I looked in upon him while he slept.

Upon the eighth night I was more than usually cautious in opening the door. A watch's minute hand moves more quickly than did mine. Never before that night had I felt the extent of my own powers—of my sagacity. I could scarcely contain my feelings of triumph. To think that there I was, opening the door, little by little, and he not even to dream of my secret deeds or thoughts. I fairly chuckled at the idea; and perhaps he heard me; for he moved on the bed suddenly, as if startled. Now you may think that I drew back—but no. His room was as black as pitch with the thick darkness, (for the shutters were close fastened, through fear of robbers,) and so I knew that he could not see the opening of the door, and I kept pushing it on steadily, steadily.

I had my head in, and was about to open the lantern, when my thumb slipped upon the tin fastening, and the old man sprang up in bed, crying out—"Who's there?"

I kept quite still and said nothing. For a whole hour I did not move a muscle, and in the meantime I did not hear him lie down. He was still sitting up in the bed listening;—just as I have done, night after night, hearkening to the death watches in the wall.

Presently I heard a slight groan, and I knew it was the groan of mortal terror. It was not a groan of pain or of grief—oh, no!—it was the low stifled sound that arises from the bottom of the soul when overcharged with awe. I knew the sound well. Many a night, just at midnight, when all the world slept, it has welled up from my own bosom, deepening, with its dreadful echo, the terrors that distracted me. I say I knew it well. I knew what the old man felt, and pitied him, although I chuckled at heart. I knew that he had been lying awake ever since the first slight noise, when he had turned in the bed. His fears had been ever since growing upon him. He had been trying to fancy them causeless, but could not. He had been saying to himself—"It is nothing but the wind in the chimney—it is only a mouse crossing the floor," or "It is merely a cricket which has made a single chirp." Yes, he had been trying to comfort himself with these suppositions: but he had found all in vain. All in vain; because Death, in approaching him had stalked with his black shadow before him, and enveloped the victim. And it was the mournful influence of the unperceived shadow that caused him to feel—although he neither saw nor heard—to feel the presence of my head within the room.

When I had waited a long time, very patiently, without hearing him lie down, I resolved to open a little—a very, very little crevice in the lantern. So I opened it—you cannot imagine how stealthily, stealthily—until, at length a simple dim ray, like the thread of the spider, shot from out the crevice and fell full upon the vulture eye.

It was open—wide, wide open—and I grew furious as I gazed upon it. I saw it with perfect distinctness—all a dull blue, with a hideous veil over it that chilled the very marrow in my bones; but I could see nothing else of the old man's face or person: for I had directed the ray as if by instinct, precisely upon the damned spot.

And have I not told you that what you mistake for madness is but over-acuteness of the sense?—now, I say, there came to my ears a low, dull, quick sound, such as a watch makes when enveloped in cotton. I knew that sound well, too. It was the beating of the old man's heart. It increased my fury, as the beating of a drum stimulates the soldier into courage.

But even yet I refrained and kept still. I scarcely breathed. I held the lantern motionless. I tried how steadily I could maintain the ray upon the eye. Meantime the hellish tattoo of the heart increased. It grew quicker and quicker, and louder and louder every instant. The old man's terror must have been extreme! It grew louder, I say, louder every moment!—do you mark me well I have told you that I am nervous: so I am. And now at the dead hour of the night, amid the dreadful silence of that old house, so strange a noise as this excited me to uncontrollable terror. Yet, for some minutes longer I refrained and stood still. But the beating grew louder, louder! I thought the heart must burst. And now a new anxiety seized me—the sound would be heard by a neighbour! The old man's hour had come! With a loud yell, I threw open the lantern and leaped into the room. He shrieked once—once only. In an instant I dragged him to the floor, and pulled the heavy bed over him. I then smiled gaily, to find the deed so far done. But, for many minutes, the heart beat on with a muffled sound. This, however, did not vex me; it would not be heard through the wall. At length it ceased. The old man was dead. I removed the bed and examined the corpse. Yes, he was stone, stone dead. I placed my hand upon the heart and held it there many minutes. There was no pulsation. He was stone dead. His eye would trouble me no more.

If still you think me mad, you will think so no longer when I describe the wise precautions I took for the concealment of the body. The night waned, and I worked hastily, but in silence. First of all I dismembered the corpse. I cut off the head and the arms and the legs.

I then took up three planks from the flooring of the chamber, and deposited all between the scantlings. I then replaced the boards so cleverly, so cunningly, that no human eye—not even his—could have detected anything wrong. There was nothing to wash out—no stain of any kind—no blood-spot whatever. I had been too wary for that. A tub had caught all—ha! ha!

When I had made an end of these labors, it was four o'clock—still dark as midnight. As the bell sounded the hour, there came a knocking at the street door. I went down to open it with a light heart,—for what had I now to fear? There entered three men, who introduced themselves, with perfect suavity, as officers of the police. A shriek had been heard by a neighbour during the night; suspicion of foul play had been aroused; information had been lodged at the police office, and they (the officers) had been deputed to search the premises.

I smiled,—for what had I to fear? I bade the gentlemen welcome. The shriek, I said, was my own in a dream. The old man, I mentioned, was absent in the country. I took my visitors all over the house. I bade them search—search well. I led them, at length, to his chamber. I showed them his treasures, secure, undisturbed. In the enthusiasm of my confidence, I brought chairs into the room, and desired them here to rest from their fatigues, while I myself, in the wild audacity of my perfect triumph, placed my own seat upon the very spot beneath which reposed the corpse of the victim.

The officers were satisfied. My manner had convinced them. I was singularly at ease. They sat, and while I answered cheerily, they chatted of familiar things. But, ere long, I felt myself getting pale and wished them gone. My head ached, and I fancied a ringing in my ears: but still they sat and still chatted. The ringing became more distinct:—It continued and became more distinct: I talked more freely to get rid of the feeling: but it continued and gained definiteness—until, at length, I found that the noise was not within my ears.

No doubt I now grew *very* pale;—but I talked more fluently, and with a heightened voice. Yet the sound increased—and what could I do? It was a low, dull, quick sound—much such a sound as a watch makes when enveloped in cotton. I gasped for breath—and yet the officers heard it not. I talked more quickly—more vehemently; but the noise steadily increased. I arose and argued about trifles, in a high key and with violent gesticulations; but the noise steadily increased. Why would they not be gone? I paced the floor to and fro with heavy strides, as if excited to fury by the observations of the men—but the noise steadily increased. Oh God! what could I do? I foamed—I raved—I swore! I swung the chair upon which I had been sitting, and grated it upon the boards, but the noise arose over all and continually increased. It grew louder—louder— louder! And still the men chatted pleasantly, and smiled. Was it possible they heard not? Almighty God!—no, no! They heard!—they suspected!— they knew!—they were making a mockery of my horror!-this I thought, and this I think. But anything was better than this agony! Anything was more tolerable than this derision! I could bear those hypocritical smiles no longer! I felt that I must scream or die! and now—again!—hark! louder! louder! louder! louder!

"Villains!" I shrieked, "dissemble no more! I admit the deed!—tear up the planks! here, here!—It is the beating of his hideous heart!"

Discussion Questions

1. Why does the narrator believe that he is not a madman?
2. Why does he continually claim that he is not mad?
3. What do you think the narrator means when he says the disease had sharpened his senses? What might the disease have been?
4. Why does the man's eye bother him? Do you think it is really the eye that bothers him or something else?
5. Why does the narrator watch the man every night for seven nights?

6. What is the purpose of the narrator being so sneaky and deliberate in his plans to kill the man when he could do it so easily at any time?
7. What do you think the narrator is hearing at the end of the story?
8. What could account for the sudden onset of paranoia he experiences as he chats with the police?
9. Point to places in the story that indicate the narrator is unreliable.
10. Why is the significance of the story's title?
11. The story obviously works as an example of good story-telling with tension and suspense. Does the story have a moral or message, as well?
12. Is the story an example of how people can be their own worst enemies? Do you believe some people with a predisposition to do wrong also have a need to get recognized, even if it means getting caught?

The Necklace
Guy de Maupassant

The girl was one of those pretty and charming young creatures who sometimes are born, as if by a slip of fate, into a family of clerks. She had no dowry, no expectations, no way of being known, understood, loved, married by any rich and distinguished man; so she let herself be married to a little clerk of the Ministry of Public Instruction.

She dressed plainly because she could not dress well, but she was unhappy as if she had really fallen from a higher station; since with women there is neither caste nor rank, for beauty, grace and charm take the place of family and birth. Natural ingenuity, instinct for what is elegant, a supple mind are their sole hierarchy, and often make of women of the people the equals of the very greatest ladies.

Mathilde suffered ceaselessly, feeling herself born to enjoy all delicacies and all luxuries. She was distressed at the poverty of her dwelling, at the bareness of the walls, at the shabby chairs, the ugliness of the curtains. All those things, of which another woman of her rank would never even have been conscious, tortured her and made her angry. The sight of the little Breton peasant who did her humble housework aroused in her despairing regrets and bewildering dreams. She thought of silent antechambers hung with Oriental tapestry, illumined by tall bronze candelabra, and of two great footmen in knee breeches who sleep in the big armchairs, made drowsy by the oppressive heat of the stove. She thought of long reception halls hung with ancient silk, of the dainty cabinets containing priceless curiosities and of the little coquettish perfumed reception rooms made for chatting at five o'clock with intimate friends, with men famous and sought after, whom all women envy and whose attention they all desire.

When she sat down to dinner, before the round table covered with a tablecloth in use three days, opposite her husband, who uncovered the soup tureen and declared with a delighted air, "Ah, the good soup! I don't know anything better than that," she thought of dainty dinners, of shining silverware, of tapestry that peopled the walls with ancient personages and with strange birds flying in the midst of a fairy forest; and she thought of delicious dishes served on marvellous plates and of the whispered gallantries to which you listen with a sphinxlike smile while you are eating the pink meat of a trout or the wings of a quail.

She had no gowns, no jewels, nothing. And she loved nothing but that. She felt made for that. She would have liked so much to please, to be envied, to be charming, to be sought after.

She had a friend, a former schoolmate at the convent, who was rich, and whom she did not like to go to see any more because she felt so sad when she came home.

But one evening her husband reached home with a triumphant air and holding a large envelope in his hand.

"There," said he, "there is something for you."

She tore the paper quickly and drew out a printed card which bore these words:

> *The Minister of Public Instruction and Madame Georges Ramponneau*
> *request the honor of M. and Madame Loisel's company at the palace of*
> *the Ministry on Monday evening, January 18th.*

Instead of being delighted, as her husband had hoped, she threw the invitation on the table crossly, muttering:

"What do you wish me to do with that?"

"Why, my dear, I thought you would be glad. You never go out, and this is such a fine opportunity. I had great trouble to get it. Everyone wants to go; it is very select, and they are not giving many invitations to clerks. The whole official world will be there."

She looked at him with an irritated glance and said impatiently:

"And what do you wish me to put on my back?"

He had not thought of that. He stammered:

"Why, the gown you go to the theatre in. It looks very well to me."

He stopped, distracted, seeing that his wife was weeping. Two great tears ran slowly from the corners of her eyes toward the corners of her mouth.

"What's the matter? What's the matter?" he answered.

By a violent effort she conquered her grief and replied in a calm voice, while she wiped her wet cheeks:

"Nothing. Only I have no gown, and, therefore, I can't go to this ball. Give your card to some colleague whose wife is better equipped than I am."

He was in despair. He resumed:

"Come, let us see, Mathilde. How much would it cost, a suitable gown, which you could use on other occasions—something very simple?"

She reflected several seconds, making her calculations and wondering also what sum she could ask without drawing on herself an immediate refusal and a frightened exclamation from the economical clerk.

Finally she replied hesitating:

"I don't know exactly, but I think I could manage it with four hundred francs."

He grew a little pale, because he was laying aside just that amount to buy a gun and treat himself to a little shooting next summer on the plain of Nanterre, with several friends who went to shoot larks there of a Sunday.

But he said:

"Very well. I will give you four hundred francs. And try to have a pretty gown."

The day of the ball drew near and Madame Loisel seemed sad, uneasy, anxious. Her frock was ready, however. Her husband said to her one evening:

"What is the matter? Come, you have seemed very queer these last three days."

And she answered:

"It annoys me not to have a single piece of jewelry, not a single ornament, nothing to put on. I shall look poverty-stricken. I would almost rather not go at all."

"You might wear natural flowers," said her husband. "They're very stylish at this time of year. For ten francs you can get two or three magnificent roses."

She was not convinced.

"No; there's nothing more humiliating than to look poor among other women who are rich."

"How stupid you are!" her husband cried. "Go look up your friend, Madame Forestier, and ask her to lend you some jewels. You're intimate enough with her to do that."

She uttered a cry of joy:

"True! I never thought of it."

The next day she went to her friend and told her of her distress.

Madame Forestier went to a wardrobe with a mirror, took out a large jewel box, brought it back, opened it and said to Madame Loisel:

"Choose, my dear."

She saw first some bracelets, then a pearl necklace, then a Venetian gold cross set with precious stones, of admirable workmanship. She tried on the ornaments before the mirror, hesitated and could not make up her mind to part with them, to give them back. She kept asking:

"Haven't you any more?"

"Why, yes. Look further; I don't know what you like."

Suddenly she discovered, in a black satin box, a superb diamond necklace, and her heart throbbed with an immoderate desire. Her hands trembled as she took it. She fastened it round her throat, outside her high-necked waist, and was lost in ecstasy at her reflection in the mirror.

Then she asked, hesitating, filled with anxious doubt:

"Will you lend me this, only this?"

"Why, yes, certainly."

She threw her arms round her friend's neck, kissed her passionately, then fled with her treasure.

The night of the ball arrived. Madame Loisel was a great success. She was prettier than any other woman present, elegant, graceful, smiling and wild with joy. All the men looked at her, asked her name, sought to be introduced. All the attaches of the Cabinet wished to waltz with her. She was remarked by the minister himself.

She danced with rapture, with passion, intoxicated by pleasure, forgetting all in the triumph of her beauty, in the glory of her success, in a sort of cloud of happiness comprised of all this homage, admiration, these awakened desires and of that sense of triumph which is so sweet to woman's heart.

She left the ball about four o'clock in the morning. Her husband had been sleeping since midnight in a little deserted anteroom with three other gentlemen whose wives were enjoying the ball.

He threw over her shoulders the wraps he had brought, the modest wraps of common life, the poverty of which contrasted with the elegance of the ball dress. She felt this and wished to escape so as not to be remarked by the other women, who were enveloping themselves in costly furs.

Loisel held her back, saying: "Wait a bit. You will catch cold outside. I will call a cab."

But she did not listen to him and rapidly descended the stairs. When they reached the street they could not find a carriage and began to look for one, shouting after the cabmen passing at a distance.

They went toward the Seine in despair, shivering with cold. At last they found on the quay one of those ancient night cabs which, as though they were ashamed to show their shabbiness during the day, are never seen round Paris until after dark.

It took them to their dwelling in the Rue des Martyrs, and sadly they mounted the stairs to their flat. All was ended for her. As to him, he reflected that he must be at the ministry at ten o'clock that morning.

She removed her wraps before the glass so as to see herself once more in all her glory. But suddenly she uttered a cry. She no longer had the necklace around her neck!

"What is the matter with you?" demanded her husband, already half undressed.

She turned distractedly toward him.

"I have—I have—I've lost Madame Forestier's necklace," she cried.

He stood up, bewildered.

"What!—how? Impossible!"

They looked among the folds of her skirt, of her cloak, in her pockets, everywhere, but did not find it.

"You're sure you had it on when you left the ball?" he asked.

"Yes, I felt it in the vestibule of the minister's house."

"But if you had lost it in the street we should have heard it fall. It must be in the cab."

"Yes, probably. Did you take his number?"

"No. And you—didn't you notice it?"

"No."

They looked, thunderstruck, at each other. At last Loisel put on his clothes.

"I shall go back on foot," said he, "over the whole route, to see whether I can find it."

He went out. She sat waiting on a chair in her ball dress, without strength to go to bed, overwhelmed, without any fire, without a thought.

Her husband returned about seven o'clock. He had found nothing.

He went to police headquarters, to the newspaper offices to offer a reward; he went to the cab companies — everywhere, in fact, whither he was urged by the least spark of hope.

She waited all day, in the same condition of mad fear before this terrible calamity.

Loisel returned at night with a hollow, pale face. He had discovered nothing.

"You must write to your friend," said he, "that you have broken the clasp of her necklace and that you are having it mended. That will give us time to turn round."

She wrote at his dictation.

At the end of a week they had lost all hope. Loisel, who had aged five years, declared:

"We must consider how to replace that ornament."

The next day they took the box that had contained it and went to the jeweler whose name was found within. He consulted his books.

"It was not I, madame, who sold that necklace; I must simply have furnished the case."

Then they went from jeweler to jeweler, searching for a necklace like the other, trying to recall it, both sick with chagrin and grief.

They found, in a shop at the Palais Royal, a string of diamonds that seemed to them exactly like the one they had lost. It was worth forty thousand francs. They could have it for thirty-six.

So they begged the jeweler not to sell it for three days yet. And they made a bargain that he should buy it back for thirty-four thousand francs, in case they should find the lost necklace before the end of February.

Loisel possessed eighteen thousand francs which his father had left him. He would borrow the rest.

He did borrow, asking a thousand francs of one, five hundred of another, five louis here, three louis there. He gave notes, took up ruinous obligations, dealt with usurers and all the race of lenders. He compromised all the rest of his life, risked signing a note without even knowing whether he could meet it; and, frightened by the trouble yet to come, by the black misery that was about to fall upon him, by the prospect of all the physical privations and moral tortures that he was to suffer, he went to get the new necklace, laying upon the jeweler's counter thirty-six thousand francs.

When Madame Loisel took back the necklace Madame Forestier said to her with a chilly manner:

"You should have returned it sooner; I might have needed it."

She did not open the case, as her friend had so much feared. If she had detected the substitution, what would she have thought, what would she have said? Would she not have taken Madame Loisel for a thief?

Thereafter Madame Loisel knew the horrible existence of the needy. She bore her part, however, with sudden heroism. That dreadful debt must be paid. She would pay it. They dismissed their servant; they changed their lodgings; they rented a garret under the roof.

She came to know what heavy housework meant and the odious cares of the kitchen. She washed the dishes, using her dainty fingers and rosy nails on greasy pots and pans. She washed the soiled linen, the shirts and the dishcloths, which she dried upon a line; she carried the slops down to the street every morning and carried up the water, stopping for breath at every landing. And dressed like a woman of the people, she went to the fruiterer, the grocer, the butcher, a basket on her arm, bargaining, meeting with impertinence, defending her miserable money, sou by sou.

Every month they had to meet some notes, renew others, obtain more time.

Her husband worked evenings, making up a tradesman's accounts, and late at night he often copied manuscript for five sous a page.

This life lasted ten years.

At the end of ten years they had paid everything, everything, with the rates of usury and the accumulations of the compound interest.

Madame Loisel looked old now. She had become the woman of impoverished households—strong and hard and rough. With frowsy hair, skirts askew and red hands, she talked loud while washing the floor with great swishes of water. But sometimes, when her husband was at the office, she sat down near the window and she thought of that gay evening of long ago, of that ball where she had been so beautiful and so admired.

What would have happened if she had not lost that necklace? Who knows? who knows? How strange and changeful is life! How small a thing is needed to make or ruin us!

But one Sunday, having gone to take a walk in the Champs Elysees to refresh herself after the labors of the week, she suddenly perceived a woman who was leading a child. It was Madame Forestier, still young, still beautiful, still charming.

Madame Loisel felt moved. Should she speak to her? Yes, certainly. And now that she had paid, she would tell her all about it. Why not?

She went up.

"Good-day, Jeanne."

The other, astonished to be familiarly addressed by this plain good-wife, did not recognize her at all and stammered:

"But—madame!—I do not know—You must have mistaken."

"No. I am Mathilde Loisel."

Her friend uttered a cry.

"Oh, my poor Mathilde! How you are changed!"

"Yes, I have had a pretty hard life, since I last saw you, and great poverty—and that because of you!"

"Of me! How so?"

"Do you remember that diamond necklace you lent me to wear at the ministerial ball?"

"Yes. Well?"

"Well, I lost it."

"What do you mean? You brought it back."

"I brought you back another exactly like it. And it has taken us ten years to pay for it. You can understand that it was not easy for us, for us who had nothing. At last it is ended, and I am very glad."

Madame Forestier had stopped.

"You say that you bought a necklace of diamonds to replace mine?"

"Yes. You never noticed it, then! They were very similar."

And she smiled with a joy that was at once proud and ingenuous.

Madame Forestier, deeply moved, took her hands.

"Oh, my poor Mathilde! Why, my necklace was paste! It was worth at most only five hundred francs!"

Discussion Questions

1. In what time period, approximately, would you guess the story takes place? What aspects of the story lead you to that assumption?
2. Why does Mathilde believe she should have been born into upper-class society?
3. Can you think of anything that might have influenced her at a young age to desire elegance?
4. Do stories like the Loisels' happen in real life? Do people with a good life lose it when trying for a better one?
5. What do people do today to try to appear wealthy?
6. What characteristics of Mathilde reflect her selfishness?
7. How does Mathilde's behavior affect her husband?
8. Why wasn't she proud of how hard her husband worked? Why wasn't she satisfied?
9. What role does irony play in this story?
10. Will Madame Forestier do anything to repay the Loisels? Would you?
11. Is Mathilde a better person after her ten-year ordeal?
12. How do the maxims "everything that glitters is not gold" and "honesty is the best policy" apply to this story?
13. How do you think the Loisels react upon hearing the news at the end of the story?
14. Is the story meant to be humorous or meant to teach a lesson?
15. Should how you dress matter?

To Build a Fire
Jack London

Day had broken cold and grey, exceedingly cold and grey, when the man turned aside from the main Yukon trail and climbed the high earth-bank, where a dim and little-travelled trail led eastward through the fat spruce timberland. It was a steep bank, and he paused for breath at the top, excusing the act to himself by looking at his watch. It was nine o'clock. There was no sun nor hint of sun, though there was not a cloud in the sky. It was a clear day, and yet there seemed an intangible pall over the face of things, a subtle gloom that made the day dark, and that was due to the absence of sun. This fact did not worry the man. He was used to the lack of sun. It had been days since he had seen the sun, and he knew that a few more days must pass before that cheerful orb, due south, would just peep above the sky-line and dip immediately from view.

The man flung a look back along the way he had come. The Yukon lay a mile wide and hidden under three feet of ice. On top of this ice were as many feet of snow. It was all pure white, rolling in gentle undulations where the ice-jams of the freeze-up had formed. North and south, as far as his eye could see, it was unbroken white, save for a dark hair-line that curved and twisted from around the spruce-covered island to the south, and that curved and twisted away into the north, where it disappeared behind another spruce-covered island. This dark hair-line was the trail—the main trail—that led south five hundred miles to the Chilcoot Pass, Dyea, and salt water; and that led north seventy miles to Dawson, and still on to the north a thousand miles to Nulato, and finally to St. Michael on Bering Sea, a thousand miles and half a thousand more.

But all this—the mysterious, far-reaching hairline trail, the absence of sun from the sky, the tremendous cold, and the strangeness and weirdness of it all—made no impression on the man. It was not because he was long used to it. He was a new-comer in the land, a *chechaquo*, and this was his first winter. The trouble with him was that he was without imagination. He was quick and alert in the things of life, but only in the things, and not in the significances. Fifty degrees below zero meant eighty odd degrees of frost. Such fact impressed him as being cold and uncomfortable, and that was all. It did not lead him to meditate upon his frailty as a creature of temperature, and upon man's frailty in general, able only to live within certain narrow limits of heat and cold; and from there on it did not lead him to the conjectural field of immortality and man's place in the universe. Fifty degrees below zero stood for a bite of frost that hurt and that must be guarded against by the use of mittens, ear-flaps, warm moccasins, and thick socks. Fifty degrees below zero was to him just precisely fifty degrees below zero. That there should be anything more to it than that was a thought that never entered his head.

As he turned to go on, he spat speculatively. There was a sharp, explosive crackle that startled him. He spat again. And again, in the air, before it could fall to the snow, the spittle crackled. He knew that at fifty below spittle crackled on the snow, but this spittle had crackled in the air. Undoubtedly it was colder than fifty below—how much colder he did not know. But the temperature did not matter. He was bound for the old claim on the left fork of Henderson Creek, where the boys were already. They had come over across the divide from the Indian Creek country, while he had come the roundabout way to take a look at the possibilities of getting out logs in the spring from the islands in the Yukon. He would be in to camp by six o'clock; a bit after dark, it was true, but the boys would be there, a fire would be going, and a hot supper would be ready. As for lunch, he pressed his hand against the protruding bundle under his jacket. It was also under his shirt, wrapped up in a handkerchief and lying against the naked skin. It was the only way to keep the biscuits from freezing. He smiled agreeably to himself as he thought of those biscuits, each cut open and sopped in bacon grease, and each enclosing a generous slice of fried bacon.

He plunged in among the big spruce trees. The trail was faint. A foot of snow had fallen since the last sled had passed over, and he was glad he was without a sled, travelling light. In fact, he carried nothing but the lunch wrapped in the handkerchief. He was surprised, however, at the cold. It certainly was cold, he concluded, as he rubbed his numbed nose and cheek-bones with his mittened hand. He was a warm-whiskered man, but the hair on his face did not protect the high cheek-bones and the eager nose that thrust itself aggressively into the frosty air.

At the man's heels trotted a dog, a big native husky, the proper wolf-dog, grey-coated and without any visible or temperamental difference from its brother, the wild wolf. The animal was depressed by the tremendous cold. It knew that it was no time for travelling. Its instinct told it a truer tale than was told to the man by the man's judgment. In reality, it was not merely colder than fifty below zero; it was colder than sixty below, than seventy below. It was seventy-five below zero. Since the freezing-point is thirty-two above zero, it meant that one hundred and seven degrees of frost obtained. The dog did not know anything about thermometers. Possibly in its brain there was no sharp consciousness of a condition of very cold such as was in the man's brain. But the brute had its instinct. It experienced a vague but menacing apprehension that subdued it and made it slink along at the man's heels, and that made it question eagerly every unwonted movement of the man as if expecting him to go into camp or to seek shelter somewhere and build a fire. The dog had learned fire, and it wanted fire, or else to burrow under the snow and cuddle its warmth away from the air.

The frozen moisture of its breathing had settled on its fur in a fine powder of frost, and especially were its jowls, muzzle, and eyelashes

17

whitened by its crystalled breath. The man's red beard and moustache were likewise frosted, but more solidly, the deposit taking the form of ice and increasing with every warm, moist breath he exhaled. Also, the man was chewing tobacco, and the muzzle of ice held his lips so rigidly that he was unable to clear his chin when he expelled the juice. The result was that a crystal beard of the colour and solidity of amber was increasing its length on his chin. If he fell down it would shatter itself, like glass, into brittle fragments. But he did not mind the appendage. It was the penalty all tobacco-chewers paid in that country, and he had been out before in two cold snaps. They had not been so cold as this, he knew, but by the spirit thermometer at Sixty Mile he knew they had been registered at fifty below and at fifty-five.

He held on through the level stretch of woods for several miles, crossed a wide flat of nigger-heads, and dropped down a bank to the frozen bed of a small stream. This was Henderson Creek, and he knew he was ten miles from the forks. He looked at his watch. It was ten o'clock. He was making four miles an hour, and he calculated that he would arrive at the forks at half-past twelve. He decided to celebrate that event by eating his lunch there.

The dog dropped in again at his heels, with a tail drooping discouragement, as the man swung along the creek-bed. The furrow of the old sled-trail was plainly visible, but a dozen inches of snow covered the marks of the last runners. In a month no man had come up or down that silent creek. The man held steadily on. He was not much given to thinking, and just then particularly he had nothing to think about save that he would eat lunch at the forks and that at six o'clock he would be in camp with the boys. There was nobody to talk to and, had there been, speech would have been impossible because of the ice-muzzle on his mouth. So he continued monotonously to chew tobacco and to increase the length of his amber beard.

Once in a while the thought reiterated itself that it was very cold and that he had never experienced such cold. As he walked along he rubbed his cheek-bones and nose with the back of his mittened hand. He did this automatically, now and again changing hands. But rub as he would, the instant he stopped his cheek-bones went numb, and the following instant the end of his nose went numb. He was sure to frost his cheeks; he knew that, and experienced a pang of regret that he had not devised a nose-strap of the sort Bud wore in cold snaps. Such a strap passed across the cheeks, as well, and saved them. But it didn't matter much, after all. What were frosted cheeks? A bit painful, that was all; they were never serious.

Empty as the man's mind was of thoughts, he was keenly observant, and he noticed the changes in the creek, the curves and bends and timber-jams, and always he sharply noted where he placed his feet. Once, coming around a bend, he shied abruptly, like a startled horse, curved away from the place where he had been walking, and retreated several paces back along the trail. The creek he knew was frozen clear to the bottom—no creek could contain water in that arctic winter—but he knew also that there were springs that bubbled out from the hillsides and ran along under the snow and on top the ice of the creek. He knew that the coldest snaps never froze these springs, and he knew likewise their danger. They were traps. They hid pools of water under the snow that might be three inches deep, or three feet. Sometimes a skin of ice half an inch thick covered them, and in turn was covered by the snow. Sometimes there were alternate layers of water and ice-skin, so that when one broke through he kept on breaking through for a while, sometimes wetting himself to the waist.

That was why he had shied in such panic. He had felt the give under his feet and heard the crackle of a snow-hidden ice-skin. And to get his feet wet in such a temperature meant trouble and danger. At the very least it meant delay, for he would be forced to stop and build a fire, and under its protection to bare his feet while he dried his socks and moccasins. He stood and studied the creek-bed and its banks, and decided that the flow of water came from the right. He reflected awhile, rubbing his nose and cheeks, then skirted to the left, stepping gingerly and testing the footing for each step. Once clear of the danger, he took a fresh chew of tobacco and swung along at his four-mile gait.

In the course of the next two hours he came upon several similar traps. Usually the snow above the hidden pools had a sunken, candied appearance that advertised the danger. Once again, however, he had a close call; and once, suspecting danger, he compelled the dog to go on in front. The dog did not want to go. It hung back until the man shoved it forward, and then it went quickly across the white, unbroken surface. Suddenly it broke through, floundered to one side, and got away to firmer footing. It had wet its forefeet and legs, and almost immediately the water that clung to it turned to ice. It made quick efforts to lick the ice off its legs, then dropped down in the snow and began to bite out the ice that had formed between the toes. This was a matter of instinct. To permit the ice to remain would mean sore feet. It did not know this. It merely obeyed the mysterious prompting that arose from the deep crypts of its being. But the man knew, having achieved a judgment on the subject, and he removed the mitten from his right hand and helped tear out the ice-particles. He did not expose his fingers more than a minute, and was astonished at the swift numbness that smote them. It certainly was cold. He pulled on the mitten hastily, and beat the hand savagely across his chest.

At twelve o'clock the day was at its brightest. Yet the sun was too far south on its winter journey to clear the horizon. The bulge of the earth intervened between it and Henderson Creek, where the man walked under a clear sky at noon and cast no shadow. At half-past twelve, to the minute, he arrived at the forks of the creek. He was pleased at the speed he had made. If he kept it up, he would certainly be with the boys by six. He unbuttoned his jacket and shirt and drew forth his lunch. The action consumed no more than a quarter of a minute, yet in that brief moment the numbness laid hold of the exposed fingers. He did not put the mitten on, but, instead, struck the fingers a dozen sharp smashes against his leg. Then he sat down on a snow-covered log to eat. The sting that followed upon the striking of his fingers against his leg ceased so quickly that he was startled, he had had no chance to take a bite of biscuit. He struck the fingers repeatedly and returned them to the mitten, baring the other hand for the purpose of eating. He tried to take a mouthful, but the ice-muzzle prevented. He had forgotten to build a fire and thaw out. He chuckled at his foolishness, and as he chuckled he noted the numbness creeping into the exposed fingers. Also, he noted that the stinging which had first come to his toes when he sat down was already passing away. He wondered whether the toes were warm or numbed. He moved them inside the moccasins and decided that they were numbed.

He pulled the mitten on hurriedly and stood up. He was a bit frightened. He stamped up and down until the stinging returned into the feet. It certainly was cold, was his thought. That man from Sulphur Creek had spoken the truth when telling how cold it sometimes got in the country. And he had laughed at him at the time! That showed one must not be too sure of things. There was no mistake about it, it was cold. He strode up and down, stamping his feet and threshing his arms, until reassured by the returning warmth. Then he got out matches and proceeded to make a fire. From the undergrowth, where high water of the previous spring had lodged a supply of seasoned twigs, he got his firewood. Working carefully from a small beginning, he soon had a roaring fire, over which he thawed the ice from his face and in the protection of which he ate his biscuits. For the moment the cold of space was outwitted. The dog took satisfaction in the fire, stretching out close enough for warmth and far enough away to escape being singed.

When the man had finished, he filled his pipe and took his comfortable time over a smoke. Then he pulled on his mittens, settled the ear-flaps of his cap firmly about his ears, and took the creek trail up the left fork. The dog was disappointed and yearned back toward the fire. This man did not know cold. Possibly all the generations of his ancestry had been ignorant of cold, of real cold, of cold one hundred and seven degrees below freezing-point. But the dog knew; all its ancestry knew, and it had inherited the knowledge. And it knew that it was not good to walk abroad in such fearful cold. It was the time to lie snug in a hole in the snow and wait for a curtain of cloud to be drawn across the face of outer space whence this cold came. On the other hand, there was keen intimacy between the dog and the man. The one was the toil-slave of the other, and the only caresses it had ever received were the caresses of the whip-lash and of harsh and menacing throat-sounds that threatened the whip-lash.

So the dog made no effort to communicate its apprehension to the man. It was not concerned in the welfare of the man; it was for its own sake that it yearned back toward the fire. But the man whistled, and spoke to it with the sound of whip-lashes, and the dog swung in at the man's heels and followed after.

The man took a chew of tobacco and proceeded to start a new amber beard. Also, his moist breath quickly powdered with white his moustache, eyebrows, and lashes. There did not seem to be so many springs on the left fork of the Henderson, and for half an hour the man saw no signs of any. And then it happened. At a place where there were no signs, where the soft, unbroken snow seemed to advertise solidity beneath, the man broke through. It was not deep. He wetted himself half-way to the knees before he floundered out to the firm crust.

He was angry, and cursed his luck aloud. He had hoped to get into camp with the boys at six o'clock, and this would delay him an hour, for he would have to build a fire and dry out his foot-gear. This was imperative at that low temperature—he knew that much; and he turned aside to the bank, which he climbed. On top, tangled in the underbrush about the trunks of several small spruce trees, was a high-water deposit of dry firewood—sticks and twigs principally, but also larger portions of seasoned branches and fine, dry, last-year's grasses. He threw down several large pieces on top of the snow. This served for a foundation and prevented the young flame from drowning itself in the snow it otherwise would melt. The flame he got by touching a match to a small shred of birch-bark that he took from his pocket. This burned even more readily than paper. Placing it on the foundation, he fed the young flame with wisps of dry grass and with the tiniest dry twigs.

He worked slowly and carefully, keenly aware of his danger. Gradually, as the flame grew stronger, he increased the size of the twigs with which he fed it. He squatted in the snow, pulling the twigs out from their entanglement in the brush and feeding directly to the flame. He knew there must be no failure. When it is seventy-five below zero, a man must not fail in his first attempt to build a fire—that is, if his feet are wet. If his feet are dry, and he fails, he can run along the trail for half a mile and restore his circulation. But the circulation of wet and freezing feet cannot be restored by running when it is seventy-five below. No matter how fast he runs, the wet feet will freeze the harder.

All this the man knew. The old-timer on Sulphur Creek had told him about it the previous fall, and now he was appreciating the advice. Already all sensation had gone out of his feet. To build the fire he had been forced to remove his mittens, and the fingers had quickly gone numb. His pace of four miles an hour had kept his heart pumping blood to the surface of his body and to all the extremities. But the instant he stopped, the action of the pump eased down. The cold of space smote the unprotected tip of the planet, and he, being on that unprotected tip, received the full force of the blow. The blood of his body recoiled before it. The blood was alive, like the dog, and like the dog it wanted to hide away and cover itself up from the fearful cold. So long as he walked four miles an hour, he pumped that blood, willy-nilly, to the surface; but now it ebbed away and sank down into the recesses of his body. The extremities were the first to feel its absence. His wet feet froze the faster, and his exposed fingers numbed the faster, though they had not yet begun to freeze. Nose and cheeks were already freezing, while the skin of all his body chilled as it lost its blood.

But he was safe. Toes and nose and cheeks would be only touched by the frost, for the fire was beginning to burn with strength. He was feeding it with twigs the size of his finger. In another minute he would be able to feed it with branches the size of his wrist, and then he could remove his wet foot-gear, and, while it dried, he could keep his naked feet warm by the fire, rubbing them at first, of course, with snow. The fire was a success. He was safe. He remembered the advice of the old-timer on Sulphur Creek, and smiled. The old-timer had been very serious in laying down the law that no man must travel alone in the Klondike after fifty below. Well, here he was; he had had the accident; he was alone; and he had saved himself. Those old-timers were rather womanish, some of them, he thought. All a man had to do was to keep his head, and he was all right. Any man who was a man could travel alone. But it was surprising, the rapidity with which his cheeks and nose were freezing. And he had not thought his fingers could go lifeless in so short a time. Lifeless they were, for he could scarcely make them move together to grip a twig, and they seemed remote from his body and from him. When he touched a twig, he had to look and see whether or not he had hold of it. The wires were pretty well down between him and his finger-ends.

All of which counted for little. There was the fire, snapping and crackling and promising life with every dancing flame. He started to untie his moccasins. They were coated with ice; the thick German socks were like sheaths of iron half-way to the knees; and the mocassin strings were like rods of steel all twisted and knotted as by some conflagration. For a moment he tugged with his numbed fingers, then, realizing the folly of it, he drew his sheath-knife.

But before he could cut the strings, it happened. It was his own fault or, rather, his mistake. He should not have built the fire under the spruce tree. He should have built it in the open. But it had been easier to pull the twigs from the brush and drop them directly on the fire. Now the tree under which he had done this carried a weight of snow on its boughs. No wind had blown for weeks, and each bough was fully freighted. Each time he had pulled a twig he had communicated a slight agitation to the tree— an imperceptible agitation, so far as he was concerned, but an agitation sufficient to bring about the disaster. High up in the tree one bough capsized its load of snow. This fell on the boughs beneath, capsizing them. This process continued, spreading out and involving the whole tree. It grew like an avalanche, and it descended without warning upon the man and the fire, and the fire was blotted out! Where it had burned was a mantle of fresh and disordered snow.

The man was shocked. It was as though he had just heard his own sentence of death. For a moment he sat and stared at the spot where the fire had been. Then he grew very calm. Perhaps the old-timer on Sulphur Creek was right. If he had only had a trail-mate he would have been in no danger now. The trail-mate could have built the fire. Well, it was up to him to build the fire over again, and this second time there must be no failure. Even if he succeeded, he would most likely lose some toes. His feet must be badly frozen by now, and there would be some time before the second fire was ready.

Such were his thoughts, but he did not sit and think them. He was busy all the time they were passing through his mind, he made a new foundation for a fire, this time in the open; where no treacherous tree could blot it out. Next, he gathered dry grasses and tiny twigs from the high-water flotsam. He could not bring his fingers together to pull them out, but he was able to gather them by the handful. In this way he got many rotten twigs and bits of green moss that were undesirable, but it was the best he could do. He worked methodically, even collecting an armful of the larger branches to be used later when the fire gathered strength. And all the while the dog sat and watched him, a certain yearning wistfulness in its eyes, for it looked upon him as the fire-provider, and the fire was slow in coming.

When all was ready, the man reached in his pocket for a second piece of birch-bark. He knew the bark was there, and, though he could not feel it with his fingers, he could hear its crisp rustling as he fumbled for it. Try as he would, he could not clutch hold of it. And all the time, in his consciousness, was the knowledge that each instant his feet were freezing. This thought tended to put him in a panic, but he fought against it and kept calm. He pulled on his mittens with his teeth, and threshed his arms back and forth, beating his hands with all his might against his sides. He did this sitting down, and he stood up to do it; and all the while the dog sat in the snow, its wolf-brush of a tail curled around warmly over its forefeet, its sharp wolf-ears pricked forward intently as it watched the man. And the man as he beat and threshed with his arms and hands, felt a great surge of envy as he regarded the creature that was warm and secure in its natural covering.

After a time he was aware of the first far-away signals of sensation in his beaten fingers. The faint tingling grew stronger till it evolved into a stinging ache that was excruciating, but which the man hailed with satisfaction. He stripped the mitten from his right hand and fetched forth the birch-bark. The exposed fingers were quickly going numb again. Next he brought out his bunch of sulphur matches. But the tremendous cold had already driven the life out of his fingers. In his effort to separate one match from the others, the whole bunch fell in the snow. He tried to pick it out of the snow, but failed. The dead fingers could neither touch nor clutch. He was very careful. He drove the thought of his freezing feet, and nose, and cheeks, out of his mind, devoting his whole soul to the matches. He watched, using the sense of vision in place of that of touch, and when he saw his fingers on each side the bunch, he closed them—that is, he willed to close them, for the wires were drawn, and the fingers did not obey. He pulled the mitten on the right hand, and beat it fiercely against his knee. Then, with both mittened hands, he scooped the bunch of matches, along with much snow, into his lap. Yet he was no better off.

After some manipulation he managed to get the bunch between the heels of his mittened hands. In this fashion he carried it to his mouth. The ice crackled and snapped when by a violent effort he opened his mouth. He drew the lower jaw in, curled the upper lip out of the way, and scraped the bunch with his upper teeth in order to separate a match. He succeeded in getting one, which he dropped on his lap. He was no better off. He could not pick it up. Then he devised a way. He picked it up in his teeth and scratched it on his leg. Twenty times he scratched before he succeeded in lighting it. As it flamed he held it with his teeth to the birch-bark. But the burning brimstone went up his nostrils and into his lungs, causing him to cough spasmodically. The match fell into the snow and went out.

The old-timer on Sulphur Creek was right, he thought in the moment of controlled despair that ensued: after fifty below, a man should travel with a partner. He beat his hands, but failed in exciting any sensation. Suddenly he bared both hands, removing the mittens with his teeth. He caught the whole bunch between the heels of his hands. His arm-muscles not being frozen enabled him to press the hand-heels tightly against the matches. Then he scratched the bunch along his leg. It flared into flame, seventy sulphur matches at once! There was no wind to blow them out. He kept his head to one side to escape the strangling fumes, and held the blazing bunch to the birch-bark. As he so held it, he became aware of sensation in his hand. His flesh was burning. He could smell it. Deep down below the surface he could feel it. The sensation developed into pain that grew acute. And still he endured it, holding the flame of the matches clumsily to the bark that would not light readily because his own burning hands were in the way, absorbing most of the flame.

At last, when he could endure no more, he jerked his hands apart. The blazing matches fell sizzling into the snow, but the birch-bark was alight. He began laying dry grasses and the tiniest twigs on the flame. He could not pick and choose, for he had to lift the fuel between the heels of his hands. Small pieces of rotten wood and green moss clung to the twigs, and he bit them off as well as he could with his teeth. He cherished the flame carefully and awkwardly. It meant life, and it must not perish. The withdrawal of blood from the surface of his body now made him begin to shiver, and he grew more awkward. A large piece of green moss fell squarely on the little fire. He tried to poke it out with his fingers, but his shivering frame made him poke too far, and he disrupted the nucleus of the little fire, the burning grasses and tiny twigs separating and scattering. He tried to poke them together again, but in spite of the tenseness of the effort, his shivering got away with him, and the twigs were hopelessly scattered. Each twig gushed a puff of smoke and went out. The fire-provider had failed. As he looked apathetically about him, his eyes chanced on the dog, sitting across the ruins of the fire from him, in the snow, making restless, hunching movements, slightly lifting one forefoot and then the other, shifting its weight back and forth on them with wistful eagerness.

The sight of the dog put a wild idea into his head. He remembered the tale of the man, caught in a blizzard, who killed a steer and crawled inside the carcass, and so was saved. He would kill the dog and bury his hands in the warm body until the numbness went out of them. Then he could build another fire. He spoke to the dog, calling it to him; but in his voice was a strange note of fear that frightened the animal, who had never known the man to speak in such way before. Something was the matter, and its suspicious nature sensed danger,—it knew not what danger but somewhere, somehow, in its brain arose an apprehension of the man. It flattened its ears down at the sound of the man's voice, and its restless, hunching movements and the liftings and shiftings of its forefeet became more pronounced but it would not come to the man. He got on his hands and knees and crawled toward the dog. This unusual posture again excited suspicion, and the animal sidled mincingly away.

The man sat up in the snow for a moment and struggled for calmness. Then he pulled on his mittens, by means of his teeth, and got upon his feet. He glanced down at first in order to assure himself that he was really standing up, for the absence of sensation in his feet left him unrelated to the earth. His erect position in itself started to drive the webs of suspicion from the dog's mind; and when he spoke peremptorily, with the sound of whip-lashes in his voice, the dog rendered its customary allegiance and came to him. As it came within reaching distance, the man lost his control. His arms flashed out to the dog, and he experienced genuine surprise when he discovered that his hands could not clutch, that there was neither bend nor feeling in the lingers. He had forgotten for the moment that they were frozen and that they were freezing more and more. All this happened quickly, and before the animal could get away, he encircled its body with his arms. He sat down in the snow, and in this fashion held the dog, while it snarled and whined and struggled.

But it was all he could do, hold its body encircled in his arms and sit there. He realized that he could not kill the dog. There was no way to do it. With his helpless hands he could neither draw nor hold his sheath-knife nor throttle the animal. He released it, and it plunged wildly away, with tail between its legs, and still snarling. It halted forty feet away and surveyed him curiously, with ears sharply pricked forward. The man looked down at his hands in order to locate them, and found them hanging on the ends of his arms. It struck him as curious that one should have to use his eyes in order to find out where his hands were. He began threshing his arms back and forth, beating the mittened hands against his sides. He did this for five minutes, violently, and his heart pumped enough blood up to the surface to put a stop to his shivering. But no sensation was aroused in the hands. He had an impression that they hung like weights on the ends of his arms, but when he tried to run the impression down, he could not find it.

A certain fear of death, dull and oppressive, came to him. This fear quickly became poignant as he realized that it was no longer a mere matter of freezing his fingers and toes, or of losing his hands and feet, but that it was a matter of life and death with the chances against him. This threw him into a panic, and he turned and ran up the creek-bed along the old, dim trail. The dog joined in behind and kept up with him. He ran blindly, without intention, in fear such as he had never known in his life. Slowly, as he ploughed and floundered through the snow, he began to see things again—the banks of the creek, the old timber-jams, the leafless aspens, and the sky. The running made him feel better. He did not shiver. Maybe, if he ran on, his feet would thaw out; and, anyway, if he ran far enough, he would reach camp and the boys. Without doubt he would lose some fingers and toes and some of his face; but the boys would take care of him, and save the rest of him when he got there. And at the same time there was another thought in his mind that said he would never get to the camp and the boys; that it was too many miles away, that the freezing had too great a start on him, and that he would soon be stiff and dead. This thought he kept in the background and refused to consider. Sometimes it pushed itself forward and demanded to be heard, but he thrust it back and strove to think of other things.

It struck him as curious that he could run at all on feet so frozen that he could not feel them when they struck the earth and took the weight of his body. He seemed to himself to skim along above the surface and to have no connection with the earth. Somewhere he had once seen a winged Mercury, and he wondered if Mercury felt as he felt when skimming over the earth.

His theory of running until he reached camp and the boys had one flaw in it: he lacked the endurance. Several times he stumbled, and finally he tottered, crumpled up, and fell. When he tried to rise, he failed. He must sit and rest, he decided, and next time he would merely walk and keep on going. As he sat and regained his breath, he noted that he was feeling quite warm and comfortable. He was not shivering, and it even seemed that a warm glow had come to his chest and trunk. And yet, when he touched his nose or cheeks, there was no sensation. Running would not thaw them out. Nor would it thaw out his hands and feet. Then the thought came to him that the frozen portions of his body must be extending. He tried to keep this thought down, to forget it, to think of something else; he was aware of the panicky feeling that it caused, and he was afraid of the panic. But the thought asserted itself, and persisted, until it produced a vision of his body totally frozen. This was too much, and he made another wild run along the trail. Once he slowed down to a walk, but the thought of the freezing extending itself made him run again.

And all the time the dog ran with him, at his heels. When he fell down a second time, it curled its tail over its forefeet and sat in front of him facing him curiously eager and intent. The warmth and security of the animal angered him, and he cursed it till it flattened down its ears appeasingly. This time the shivering came more quickly upon the man. He was losing in his battle with the frost. It was creeping into his body from all sides. The thought of it drove him on, but he ran no more than a hundred feet, when he staggered and pitched headlong. It was his last panic. When he had recovered his breath and control, he sat up and entertained in his mind the conception of meeting death with dignity. However, the conception did not come to him in such terms. His idea of it was that he had been making a fool of himself, running around like a chicken with its head cut off—such was the simile that occurred to him. Well, he was bound to freeze anyway, and he might as well take it decently. With this new-found peace of mind came the first glimmerings of drowsiness. A good idea, he thought, to sleep off to death. It was like taking an anæsthetic. Freezing was not so bad as people thought. There were lots worse ways to die.

He pictured the boys finding his body next day. Suddenly he found himself with them, coming along the trail and looking for himself. And, still with them, he came around a turn in the trail and found himself lying in the snow. He did not belong with himself any more, for even then he was out of himself, standing with the boys and looking at himself in the snow. It certainly was cold, was his thought. When he got back to the States he could tell the folks what real cold was. He drifted on from this to a vision of the old-timer on Sulphur Creek. He could see him quite clearly, warm and comfortable, and smoking a pipe.

"You were right, old hoss; you were right," the man mumbled to the old-timer of Sulphur Creek.

Then the man drowsed off into what seemed to him the most comfortable and satisfying sleep he had ever known. The dog sat facing him and waiting. The brief day drew to a close in a long, slow twilight. There were no signs of a fire to be made, and, besides, never in the dog's experience had it known a man to sit like that in the snow and make no fire. As the twilight drew on, its eager yearning for the fire mastered it, and with a great lifting and shifting of forefeet, it whined softly, then flattened its ears down in anticipation of being chidden by the man. But the man remained silent. Later, the dog whined loudly. And still later it crept close to the man and caught the scent of death. This made the animal bristle and back away. A little longer it delayed, howling under the stars that leaped and danced and shone brightly in the cold sky. Then it turned and trotted up the trail in the direction of the camp it knew, where were the other food-providers and fire-providers.

Discussion Questions

1. Why does the author not give the man or the dog a name?
2. Why doesn't the man worry more about the cold and the frostbite? Why does he believe he doesn't need a companion?
3. How would you describe the man's relationship with the dog?
4. Had the man taken note of the dog's temperament, might things have turned out differently?
5. What role does setting play in the story?
6. How does the man's attitude change as the story progresses?
7. How does the author use the old-timer of Sulphur Creek to illustrate the change in the man's thinking?
8. At what point does the man realize the seriousness of his situation?
9. Do you believe more supplies could have saved the man's life, or was his fate sealed the moment he left alone?
10. Does the man's perception of "manliness" play a role in his fate?
11. What character traits would have been useful to the narrator in this story?
12. If you had to sum up the man's fatal flaw in one word, what word would you choose?
13. Does the story have modern implications? Are there situations today in which mankind might be lacking imagination?

Miss Brill
Katherine Mansfield

Although it was so brilliantly fine—the blue sky powdered with gold and great spots of light like white wine splashed over the Jardins Publiques—Miss Brill was glad that she had decided on her fur. The air was motionless, but when you opened your mouth there was just a faint chill, like a chill from a glass of iced water before you sip, and now and again a leaf came drifting—from nowhere, from the sky. Miss Brill put up her hand and touched her fur. Dear little thing! It was nice to feel it again. She had taken it out of its box that afternoon, shaken out the moth-powder, given it a good brush, and rubbed the life back into the dim little eyes. "What has been happening to me?" said the sad little eyes. Oh, how sweet it was to see them snap at her again from the red eiderdown!... But the nose, which was of some black composition, wasn't at all firm. It must have had a knock, somehow. Never mind—a little dab of black sealing-wax when the time came—when it was absolutely necessary... Little rogue! Yes, she really felt like that about it. Little rogue biting its tail just by her left ear. She could have taken it off and laid it on her lap and stroked it. She felt a tingling in her hands and arms, but that came from walking, she supposed. And when she breathed, something light and sad—no, not sad, exactly—something gentle seemed to move in her bosom.

There were a number of people out this afternoon, far more than last Sunday. And the band sounded louder and gayer. That was because the Season had begun. For although the band played all the year round on Sundays, out of season it was never the same. It was like someone playing with only the family to listen; it didn't care how it played if there weren't any strangers present. Wasn't the conductor wearing a new coat, too? She was sure it was new. He scraped with his foot and flapped his arms like a rooster about to crow, and the bandsmen sitting in the green rotunda blew out their cheeks and glared at the music. Now there came a little "flutey" bit—very pretty!—a little chain of bright drops. She was sure it would be repeated. It was; she lifted her head and smiled.

Only two people shared her "special" seat: a fine old man in a velvet coat, his hands clasped over a huge carved walking-stick, and a big old woman, sitting upright, with a roll of knitting on her embroidered apron. They did not speak. This was disappointing, for Miss Brill always looked forward to the conversation. She had become really quite expert, she thought, at listening as though she didn't listen, at sitting in other people's lives just for a minute while they talked round her.

She glanced, sideways, at the old couple. Perhaps they would go soon. Last Sunday, too, hadn't been as interesting as usual. An Englishman and his wife, he wearing a dreadful Panama hat and she button boots. And she'd gone on the whole time about how she ought to wear spectacles; she knew she needed them; but that it was no good getting any; they'd be sure to break and they'd never keep on. And he'd been so patient. He'd suggested everything—gold rims, the kind that curved round your ears, little pads inside the bridge. No, nothing would please her. "They'll always be sliding down my nose!" Miss Brill had wanted to shake her.

The old people sat on the bench, still as statues. Never mind, there was always the crowd to watch. To and fro, in front of the flower-beds and the band rotunda, the couples and groups paraded, stopped to talk, to greet, to buy a handful of flowers from the old beggar who had his tray fixed to the railings. Little children ran among them, swooping and laughing; little boys with big white silk bows under their chins, little girls, little French dolls, dressed up in velvet and lace. And sometimes a tiny staggerer came suddenly rocking into the open from under the trees, stopped, stared, as suddenly sat down "flop," until its small high-stepping mother, like a young hen, rushed scolding to its rescue. Other people sat on the benches and green chairs, but they were nearly always the same, Sunday after Sunday, and—Miss Brill had often noticed—there was something funny about nearly all of them. They were odd, silent, nearly all old, and from the way they stared they looked as though they'd just come from dark little rooms or even—even cupboards!

Behind the rotunda the slender trees with yellow leaves down drooping, and through them just a line of sea, and beyond the blue sky with gold-veined clouds.

Tum-tum-tum tiddle-um! tiddle-um! tum tiddley-um tum ta! blew the band.

Two young girls in red came by and two young soldiers in blue met them, and they laughed and paired and went off arm-in-arm. Two peasant women with funny straw hats passed, gravely, leading beautiful smoke-coloured donkeys. A cold, pale nun hurried by. A beautiful woman came along and dropped her bunch of violets, and a little boy ran after to hand them to her, and she took them and threw them away as if they'd been poisoned. Dear me! Miss Brill didn't know whether to admire that or not! And now an ermine toque and a gentleman in grey met just in front of her. He was tall, stiff, dignified, and she was wearing the ermine toque she'd bought when her hair was yellow. Now everything, her hair, her face, even her eyes, was the same colour as the shabby ermine, and her hand, in its cleaned glove, lifted to dab her lips, was a tiny yellowish paw. Oh, she was so pleased to see him—delighted! She rather thought they were going to meet that afternoon. She described where she'd been—everywhere, here, there, along by the sea. The day was so charming—didn't he agree? And wouldn't he, perhaps?... But he shook his head, lighted a cigarette, slowly breathed a great deep puff into her face, and even while she was still talking and laughing, flicked the match away and walked on. The ermine toque was alone; she smiled more brightly than ever. But even the band seemed to know what she was feeling and played more softly, played tenderly, and the drum beat, "The Brute! The Brute!"

over and over. What would she do? What was going to happen now? But as Miss Brill wondered, the ermine toque turned, raised her hand as though she'd seen someone else, much nicer, just over there, and pattered away. And the band changed again and played more quickly, more gayly than ever, and the old couple on Miss Brill's seat got up and marched away, and such a funny old man with long whiskers hobbled along in time to the music and was nearly knocked over by four girls walking abreast.

Oh, how fascinating it was! How she enjoyed it! How she loved sitting here, watching it all! It was like a play. It was exactly like a play. Who could believe the sky at the back wasn't painted? But it wasn't till a little brown dog trotted on solemn and then slowly trotted off, like a little "theatre" dog, a little dog that had been drugged, that Miss Brill discovered what it was that made it so exciting. They were all on the stage. They weren't only the audience, not only looking on; they were acting. Even she had a part and came every Sunday. No doubt somebody would have noticed if she hadn't been there; she was part of the performance after all. How strange she'd never thought of it like that before! And yet it explained why she made such a point of starting from home at just the same time each week—so as not to be late for the performance—and it also explained why she had quite a queer, shy feeling at telling her English pupils how she spent her Sunday afternoons. No wonder! Miss Brill nearly laughed out loud. She was on the stage. She thought of the old invalid gentleman to whom she read the newspaper four afternoons a week while he slept in the garden. She had got quite used to the frail head on the cotton pillow, the hollowed eyes, the open mouth and the high pinched nose. If he'd been dead she mightn't have noticed for weeks; she wouldn't have minded. But suddenly he knew he was having the paper read to him by an actress! "An actress!" The old head lifted; two points of light quivered in the old eyes. "An actress—are ye?" And Miss Brill smoothed the newspaper as though it were the manuscript of her part and said gently; "Yes, I have been an actress for a long time."

The band had been having a rest. Now they started again. And what they played was warm, sunny, yet there was just a faint chill—a something, what was it?—not sadness—no, not sadness—a something that made you want to sing. The tune lifted, lifted, the light shone; and it seemed to Miss Brill that in another moment all of them, all the whole company, would begin singing. The young ones, the laughing ones who were moving together, they would begin, and the men's voices, very resolute and brave, would join them. And then she too, she too, and the others on the benches—they would come in with a kind of accompaniment—something low, that scarcely rose or fell, something so beautiful—moving... And Miss Brill's eyes filled with tears and she looked smiling at all the other members of the company. Yes, we understand, we understand, she thought—though what they understood she didn't know.

31

Just at that moment a boy and girl came and sat down where the old couple had been. They were beautifully dressed; they were in love. The hero and heroine, of course, just arrived from his father's yacht. And still soundlessly singing, still with that trembling smile, Miss Brill prepared to listen.

"No, not now," said the girl. "Not here, I can't."

"But why? Because of that stupid old thing at the end there?" asked the boy. "Why does she come here at all—who wants her? Why doesn't she keep her silly old mug at home?"

"It's her fu-ur which is so funny," giggled the girl. "It's exactly like a fried whiting."

"Ah, be off with you!" said the boy in an angry whisper. Then: "Tell me, *ma petite chere*—"

"No, not here," said the girl. "Not yet."

On her way home she usually bought a slice of honey-cake at the baker's. It was her Sunday treat. Sometimes there was an almond in her slice, sometimes not. It made a great difference. If there was an almond it was like carrying home a tiny present—a surprise—something that might very well not have been there. She hurried on the almond Sundays and struck the match for the kettle in quite a dashing way.

But to-day she passed the baker's by, climbed the stairs, went into the little dark room—her room like a cupboard—and sat down on the red eiderdown. She sat there for a long time. The box that the fur came out of was on the bed. She unclasped the necklet quickly; quickly, without looking, laid it inside. But when she put the lid on she thought she heard something crying.

Discussion Questions

1. How would you describe Miss Brill as she is presented at the beginning of the story?
2. Katherine Mansfield spends a lot of time describing simple things throughout the story. How does this style of writing fit the story?
3. Miss Brill describes her fur almost as if it is her pet. What is the significance of the fur?
4. Why does Miss Brill enjoy listening in on the conversation of others?
5. What event is actually happening in the story? Do you think it is as Miss Brill describes it?
6. How does coming to believe that she is part of a play—an actress—affect Miss Brill? What does she view differently after coming to this "realization"?
7. What does she mean when she adds, "Yes, I have been an actress for a long time"?

8. When the young couple first appear and sit next to her, Miss Brill in her enthusiasm over her imagined play refers to them as "the hero and heroine." After what happens, how would you describe them?

9. Do you believe the young man has a reason to insult her? Do you feel others at the event shared his view?

10. If you were Miss Brill, how would you feel upon hearing the young man's words?

11. What does the anecdote about the cake, her Sunday treat, reveal about Miss Brill? Why won't she have one this time?

12. When she puts the fur in the box at the end, she thinks she hears something cry. What is she hearing?

13. Do you think she will ever take the fur out of the box again? Why or why not?

14. How would you describe Miss Brill as she is presented at the story's conclusion?

15. Do you think Miss Brill ever went back to the event?

16. Why do you think Katherine Mansfield chose not to reveal Miss Brill's first name but instead refers to her as Miss Brill throughout the story and even the title?

Misery
Anton Chekhov

"To Whom Shall I Tell My Grief?"

THE twilight of evening. Big flakes of wet snow are whirling lazily about the street lamps, which have just been lighted, and lying in a thin soft layer on roofs, horses' backs, shoulders, caps. Iona Potapov, the sledge-driver, is all white like a ghost. He sits on the box without stirring, bent as double as the living body can be bent. If a regular snowdrift fell on him it seems as though even then he would not think it necessary to shake it off.... His little mare is white and motionless too. Her stillness, the angularity of her lines, and the stick-like straightness of her legs make her look like a halfpenny gingerbread horse. She is probably lost in thought. Anyone who has been torn away from the plough, from the familiar gray landscapes, and cast into this slough, full of monstrous lights, of unceasing uproar and hurrying people, is bound to think.

It is a long time since Iona and his nag have budged. They came out of the yard before dinnertime and not a single fare yet. But now the shades of evening are falling on the town. The pale light of the street lamps changes to a vivid color, and the bustle of the street grows noisier.

"Sledge to Vyborgskaya!" Iona hears. "Sledge!"

Iona starts, and through his snow-plastered eyelashes sees an officer in a military overcoat with a hood over his head.

"To Vyborgskaya," repeats the officer. "Are you asleep? To Vyborgskaya!"

In token of assent Iona gives a tug at the reins which sends cakes of snow flying from the horse's back and shoulders. The officer gets into the sledge. The sledge-driver clicks to the horse, cranes his neck like a swan, rises in his seat, and more from habit than necessity brandishes his whip. The mare cranes her neck, too, crooks her stick-like legs, and hesitatingly sets off....

"Where are you shoving, you devil?" Iona immediately hears shouts from the dark mass shifting to and fro before him. "Where the devil are you going? Keep to the r-right!"

"You don't know how to drive! Keep to the right," says the officer angrily.

A coachman driving a carriage swears at him; a pedestrian crossing the road and brushing the horse's nose with his shoulder looks at him angrily and shakes the snow off his sleeve. Iona fidgets on the box as though he were sitting on thorns, jerks his elbows, and turns his eyes about like one possessed as though he did not know where he was or why he was there.

"What rascals they all are!" says the officer jocosely. "They are simply doing their best to run up against you or fall under the horse's feet. They must be doing it on purpose."

Iona looks as his fare and moves his lips.... Apparently he means to say something, but nothing comes but a sniff.

"What?" inquires the officer.

Iona gives a wry smile, and straining his throat, brings out huskily: "My son... er... my son died this week, sir."

"H'm! What did he die of?"

Iona turns his whole body round to his fare, and says:

"Who can tell! It must have been from fever.... He lay three days in the hospital and then he died.... God's will."

"Turn round, you devil!" comes out of the darkness. "Have you gone cracked, you old dog? Look where you are going!"

"Drive on! drive on!..." says the officer. "We shan't get there till to-morrow going on like this. Hurry up!"

The sledge-driver cranes his neck again, rises in his seat, and with heavy grace swings his whip. Several times he looks round at the officer, but the latter keeps his eyes shut and is apparently disinclined to listen. Putting his fare down at Vyborgskaya, Iona stops by a restaurant, and again sits huddled up on the box.... Again the wet snow paints him and his horse white. One hour passes, and then another....

Three young men, two tall and thin, one short and hunchbacked, come up, railing at each other and loudly stamping on the pavement with their goloshes.

"Cabby, to the Police Bridge!" the hunchback cries in a cracked voice. "The three of us,... twenty kopecks!"

Iona tugs at the reins and clicks to his horse. Twenty kopecks is not a fair price, but he has no thoughts for that. Whether it is a rouble or whether it is five kopecks does not matter to him now so long as he has a fare.... The three young men, shoving each other and using bad language, go up to the sledge, and all three try to sit down at once. The question remains to be settled: Which are to sit down and which one is to stand? After a long altercation, ill-temper, and abuse, they come to the conclusion that the hunchback must stand because he is the shortest.

"Well, drive on," says the hunchback in his cracked voice, settling himself and breathing down Iona's neck. "Cut along! What a cap you've got, my friend! You wouldn't find a worse one in all Petersburg...."

"He-he!... he-he!..." laughs Iona. "It's nothing to boast of!"

"Well, then, nothing to boast of, drive on! Are you going to drive like this all the way? Eh? Shall I give you one in the neck?"

"My head aches," says one of the tall ones. "At the Dukmasovs' yesterday Vaska and I drank four bottles of brandy between us."

"I can't make out why you talk such stuff," says the other tall one angrily. "You lie like a brute."

"Strike me dead, it's the truth!..."

"It's about as true as that a louse coughs."

"He-he!" grins Iona. "Me-er-ry gentlemen!"

"Tfoo! the devil take you!" cries the hunchback indignantly. "Will you get on, you old plague, or won't you? Is that the way to drive? Give her one with the whip. Hang it all, give it her well."

Iona feels behind his back the jolting person and quivering voice of the hunchback. He hears abuse addressed to him, he sees people, and the feeling of loneliness begins little by little to be less heavy on his heart. The hunchback swears at him, till he chokes over some elaborately whimsical string of epithets and is overpowered by his cough. His tall companions begin talking of a certain Nadyezhda Petrovna. Iona looks round at them. Waiting till there is a brief pause, he looks round once more and says:

"This week... er... my... er... son died!"

"We shall all die,..." says the hunchback with a sigh, wiping his lips after coughing. "Come, drive on! drive on! My friends, I simply cannot stand crawling like this! When will he get us there?"

"Well, you give him a little encouragement... one in the neck!"

"Do you hear, you old plague? I'll make you smart. If one stands on ceremony with fellows like you one may as well walk. Do you hear, you old dragon? Or don't you care a hang what we say?"

And Iona hears rather than feels a slap on the back of his neck.

"He-he!..." he laughs. "Merry gentlemen.... God give you health!"

"Cabman, are you married?" asks one of the tall ones.

"I? He-he! Me-er-ry gentlemen. The only wife for me now is the damp earth.... He-ho-ho!.... The grave that is!... Here my son's dead and I am alive.... It's a strange thing, death has come in at the wrong door.... Instead of coming for me it went for my son...."

And Iona turns round to tell them how his son died, but at that point the hunchback gives a faint sigh and announces that, thank God! they have arrived at last. After taking his twenty kopecks, Iona gazes for a long while after the revelers, who disappear into a dark entry. Again he is alone and again there is silence for him.... The misery which has been for a brief space eased comes back again and tears his heart more cruelly than ever. With a look of anxiety and suffering Iona's eyes stray restlessly among the crowds moving to and fro on both sides of the street: can he not find among those thousands someone who will listen to him? But the crowds flit by heedless of him and his misery.... His misery is immense, beyond all bounds. If Iona's heart were to burst and his misery to flow out, it would flood the whole world, it seems, but yet it is not seen. It has found a hiding-place in such an insignificant shell that one would not have found it with a candle by daylight....

Iona sees a house-porter with a parcel and makes up his mind to address him.

"What time will it be, friend?" he asks.

"Going on for ten.... Why have you stopped here? Drive on!"

Iona drives a few paces away, bends himself double, and gives himself up to his misery. He feels it is no good to appeal to people. But before five minutes have passed he draws himself up, shakes his head as though he feels a sharp pain, and tugs at the reins.... He can bear it no longer.

"Back to the yard!" he thinks. "To the yard!"

And his little mare, as though she knew his thoughts, falls to trotting. An hour and a half later Iona is sitting by a big dirty stove. On the stove, on the floor, and on the benches are people snoring. The air is full of smells and stuffiness. Iona looks at the sleeping figures, scratches himself, and regrets that he has come home so early....

"I have not earned enough to pay for the oats, even," he thinks. "That's why I am so miserable. A man who knows how to do his work,... who has had enough to eat, and whose horse has had enough to eat, is always at ease...."

In one of the corners a young cabman gets up, clears his throat sleepily, and makes for the water-bucket.

"Want a drink?" Iona asks him.

"Seems so."

"May it do you good.... But my son is dead, mate.... Do you hear? This week in the hospital.... It's a queer business...."

Iona looks to see the effect produced by his words, but he sees nothing. The young man has covered his head over and is already asleep. The old man sighs and scratches himself.... Just as the young man had been thirsty for water, he thirsts for speech. His son will soon have been dead a week, and he has not really talked to anybody yet.... He wants to talk of it properly, with deliberation.... He wants to tell how his son was taken ill, how he suffered, what he said before he died, how he died.... He wants to describe the funeral, and how he went to the hospital to get his son's clothes. He still has his daughter Anisya in the country.... And he wants to talk about her too.... Yes, he has plenty to talk about now. His listener ought to sigh and exclaim and lament.... It would be even better to talk to women. Though they are silly creatures, they blubber at the first word.

"Let's go out and have a look at the mare," Iona thinks. "There is always time for sleep.... You'll have sleep enough, no fear...."

He puts on his coat and goes into the stables where his mare is standing. He thinks about oats, about hay, about the weather.... He cannot think about his son when he is alone.... To talk about him with someone is possible, but to think of him and picture him is insufferable anguish....

"Are you munching?" Iona asks his mare, seeing her shining eyes. "There, munch away, munch away.... Since we have not earned enough for oats, we will eat hay.... Yes,... I have grown too old to drive.... My son ought to be driving, not I.... He was a real cabman.... He ought to have lived...."

Iona is silent for a while, and then he goes on:

"That's how it is, old girl.... Kuzma Ionitch is gone.... He said good-by to me.... He went and died for no reason.... Now, suppose you had a little

37

colt, and you were own mother to that little colt. ... And all at once that same little colt went and died.... You'd be sorry, wouldn't you?..."

The little mare munches, listens, and breathes on her master's hands. Iona is carried away and tells her all about it.

Discussion Questions:

1. How does the question "To whom shall I tell my grief?" define the story?
2. What is symbolic about the story beginning with Iona sitting still, covered in snow?
3. In what time period might the story take place?
4. Why do all the driver's passengers complain about his driving?
5. Why does Iona never whip the horse to make her go faster despite repeatedly being told to do so?
6. What effect does Chekhov create by making Iona's first words about the death of his son?
7. Why does Iona not care how much he is paid?
8. Why would Iona "thirst for speech"?
9. What does Iona mean when he says "the only wife for me now is the damp earth"?
10. Near the end of the story readers learn the ramifications of Iona not charging enough for his fares. What are they?
11. What does Chekhov achieve by making the mare the only being who will listen to Iona?

An Occurrence at Owl Creek Bridge
Ambrose Bierce

I

A man stood upon a railroad bridge in northern Alabama, looking down into the swift water twenty feet below. The man's hands were behind his back, the wrists bound with a cord. A rope closely encircled his neck. It was attached to a stout cross-timber above his head and the slack fell to the level of his knees. Some loose boards laid upon the ties supporting the rails of the railway supplied a footing for him and his executioners—two private soldiers of the Federal army, directed by a sergeant who in civil life may have been a deputy sheriff. At a short remove upon the same temporary platform was an officer in the uniform of his rank, armed. He was a captain. A sentinel at each end of the bridge stood with his rifle in the position known as "support," that is to say, vertical in front of the left shoulder, the hammer resting on the forearm thrown straight across the chest—a formal and unnatural position, enforcing an erect carriage of the body. It did not appear to be the duty of these two men to know what was occurring at the center of the bridge; they merely blockaded the two ends of the foot planking that traversed it.

Beyond one of the sentinels nobody was in sight; the railroad ran straight away into a forest for a hundred yards, then, curving, was lost to view. Doubtless there was an outpost farther along. The other bank of the stream was open ground—a gentle slope topped with a stockade of vertical tree trunks, loop-holed for rifles, with a single embrasure through which protruded the muzzle of a brass cannon commanding the bridge. Midway up the slope between the bridge and fort were the spectators—a single company of infantry in line, at "parade rest," the butts of their rifles on the ground, the barrels inclining slightly backward against the right shoulder, the hands crossed upon the stock. A lieutenant stood at the right of the line, the point of his sword upon the ground, his left hand resting upon his right. Excepting the group of four at the center of the bridge, not a man moved. The company faced the bridge, staring stonily, motionless. The sentinels, facing the banks of the stream, might have been statues to adorn the bridge. The captain stood with folded arms, silent, observing the work of his subordinates, but making no sign. Death is a dignitary who when he comes announced is to be received with formal manifestations of respect, even by those most familiar with him. In the code of military etiquette silence and fixity are forms of deference.

The man who was engaged in being hanged was apparently about thirty-five years of age. He was a civilian, if one might judge from his habit, which was that of a planter. His features were good—a straight nose, firm mouth, broad forehead, from which his long, dark hair was combed straight back, falling behind his ears to the collar of his well-fitting frock coat. He wore a moustache and pointed beard, but no whiskers; his eyes were large and dark gray, and had a kindly expression

39

which one would hardly have expected in one whose neck was in the hemp. Evidently this was no vulgar assassin. The liberal military code makes provision for hanging many kinds of persons, and gentlemen are not excluded.

The preparations being complete, the two private soldiers stepped aside and each drew away the plank upon which he had been standing. The sergeant turned to the captain, saluted and placed himself immediately behind that officer, who in turn moved apart one pace. These movements left the condemned man and the sergeant standing on the two ends of the same plank, which spanned three of the cross-ties of the bridge. The end upon which the civilian stood almost, but not quite, reached a fourth. This plank had been held in place by the weight of the captain; it was now held by that of the sergeant. At a signal from the former the latter would step aside, the plank would tilt and the condemned man go down between two ties. The arrangement commended itself to his judgment as simple and effective. His face had not been covered nor his eyes bandaged. He looked a moment at his "unsteadfast footing," then let his gaze wander to the swirling water of the stream racing madly beneath his feet. A piece of dancing driftwood caught his attention and his eyes followed it down the current. How slowly it appeared to move! What a sluggish stream!

He closed his eyes in order to fix his last thoughts upon his wife and children. The water, touched to gold by the early sun, the brooding mists under the banks at some distance down the stream, the fort, the soldiers, the piece of drift—all had distracted him. And now he became conscious of a new disturbance. Striking through the thought of his dear ones was sound which he could neither ignore nor understand, a sharp, distinct, metallic percussion like the stroke of a blacksmith's hammer upon the anvil; it had the same ringing quality. He wondered what it was, and whether immeasurably distant or nearby— it seemed both. Its recurrence was regular, but as slow as the tolling of a death knell. He awaited each new stroke with impatience and—he knew not why—apprehension. The intervals of silence grew progressively longer; the delays became maddening. With their greater infrequency the sounds increased in strength and sharpness. They hurt his ear like the trust of a knife; he feared he would shriek. What he heard was the ticking of his watch.

He unclosed his eyes and saw again the water below him. "If I could free my hands," he thought, "I might throw off the noose and spring into the stream. By diving I could evade the bullets and, swimming vigorously, reach the bank, take to the woods and get away home. My home, thank God, is as yet outside their lines; my wife and little ones are still beyond the invader's farthest advance."

As these thoughts, which have here to be set down in words, were flashed into the doomed man's brain rather than evolved from it the captain nodded to the sergeant. The sergeant stepped aside.

II

Peyton Farquhar was a well to do planter, of an old and highly respected Alabama family. Being a slave owner and like other slave owners a politician, he was naturally an original secessionist and ardently devoted to the Southern cause. Circumstances of an imperious nature, which it is unnecessary to relate here, had prevented him from taking service with that gallant army which had fought the disastrous campaigns ending with the fall of Corinth, and he chafed under the inglorious restraint, longing for the release of his energies, the larger life of the soldier, the opportunity for distinction. That opportunity, he felt, would come, as it comes to all in wartime. Meanwhile he did what he could. No service was too humble for him to perform in the aid of the South, no adventure to perilous for him to undertake if consistent with the character of a civilian who was at heart a soldier, and who in good faith and without too much qualification assented to at least a part of the frankly villainous dictum that all is fair in love and war.

One evening while Farquhar and his wife were sitting on a rustic bench near the entrance to his grounds, a gray-clad soldier rode up to the gate and asked for a drink of water. Mrs. Farquhar was only too happy to serve him with her own white hands. While she was fetching the water her husband approached the dusty horseman and inquired eagerly for news from the front.

"The Yanks are repairing the railroads," said the man, "and are getting ready for another advance. They have reached the Owl Creek bridge, put it in order and built a stockade on the north bank. The commandant has issued an order, which is posted everywhere, declaring that any civilian caught interfering with the railroad, its bridges, tunnels, or trains will be summarily hanged. I saw the order."

"How far is it to the Owl Creek bridge?" Farquhar asked.

"About thirty miles."

"Is there no force on this side of the creek?"

"Only a picket post half a mile out, on the railroad, and a single sentinel at this end of the bridge."

"Suppose a man—a civilian and student of hanging—should elude the picket post and perhaps get the better of the sentinel," said Farquhar, smiling, "what could he accomplish?"

The soldier reflected. "I was there a month ago," he replied. "I observed that the flood of last winter had lodged a great quantity of driftwood against the wooden pier at this end of the bridge. It is now dry and would burn like tinder."

The lady had now brought the water, which the soldier drank. He thanked her ceremoniously, bowed to her husband and rode away. An hour later, after nightfall, he repassed the plantation, going northward in the direction from which he had come. He was a Federal scout.

III

As Peyton Farquhar fell straight downward through the bridge he lost consciousness and was as one already dead. From this state he was awakened—ages later, it seemed to him—by the pain of a sharp pressure upon his throat, followed by a sense of suffocation. Keen, poignant agonies seemed to shoot from his neck downward through every fiber of his body and limbs. These pains appeared to flash along well defined lines of ramification and to beat with an inconceivably rapid periodicity. They seemed like streams of pulsating fire heating him to an intolerable temperature. As to his head, he was conscious of nothing but a feeling of fullness—of congestion. These sensations were unaccompanied by thought. The intellectual part of his nature was already effaced; he had power only to feel, and feeling was torment. He was conscious of motion. Encompassed in a luminous cloud, of which he was now merely the fiery heart, without material substance, he swung through unthinkable arcs of oscillation, like a vast pendulum. Then all at once, with terrible suddenness, the light about him shot upward with the noise of a loud splash; a frightful roaring was in his ears, and all was cold and dark. The power of thought was restored; he knew that the rope had broken and he had fallen into the stream. There was no additional strangulation; the noose about his neck was already suffocating him and kept the water from his lungs. To die of hanging at the bottom of a river!—the idea seemed to him ludicrous. He opened his eyes in the darkness and saw above him a gleam of light, but how distant, how inaccessible! He was still sinking, for the light became fainter and fainter until it was a mere glimmer. Then it began to grow and brighten, and he knew that he was rising toward the surface—knew it with reluctance, for he was now very comfortable. "To be hanged and drowned," he thought, "that is not so bad; but I do not wish to be shot. No; I will not be shot; that is not fair."

He was not conscious of an effort, but a sharp pain in his wrist apprised him that he was trying to free his hands. He gave the struggle his attention, as an idler might observe the feat of a juggler, without interest in the outcome. What splendid effort!—what magnificent, what superhuman strength! Ah, that was a fine endeavor! Bravo! The cord fell away; his arms parted and floated upward, the hands dimly seen on each side in the growing light. He watched them with a new interest as first one and then the other pounced upon the noose at his neck. They tore it away and thrust it fiercely aside, its undulations resembling those of a water snake. "Put it back, put it back!" He thought he shouted these words to his hands, for the undoing of the noose had been succeeded by the direst pang that he had yet experienced. His neck ached horribly; his brain was on fire, his heart, which had been fluttering faintly, gave a great leap, trying to force itself out at his mouth. His whole body was racked and wrenched with an insupportable anguish! But his disobedient hands gave

42

no heed to the command. They beat the water vigorously with quick, downward strokes, forcing him to the surface. He felt his head emerge; his eyes were blinded by the sunlight; his chest expanded convulsively, and with a supreme and crowning agony his lungs engulfed a great draught of air, which instantly he expelled in a shriek!

He was now in full possession of his physical senses. They were, indeed, preternaturally keen and alert. Something in the awful disturbance of his organic system had so exalted and refined them that they made record of things never before perceived. He felt the ripples upon his face and heard their separate sounds as they struck. He looked at the forest on the bank of the stream, saw the individual trees, the leaves and the veining of each leaf—he saw the very insects upon them: the locusts, the brilliant bodied flies, the gray spiders stretching their webs from twig to twig. He noted the prismatic colors in all the dewdrops upon a million blades of grass. The humming of the gnats that danced above the eddies of the stream, the beating of the dragon flies' wings, the strokes of the water spiders' legs, like oars which had lifted their boat—all these made audible music. A fish slid along beneath his eyes and he heard the rush of its body parting the water.

He had come to the surface facing down the stream; in a moment the visible world seemed to wheel slowly round, himself the pivotal point, and he saw the bridge, the fort, the soldiers upon the bridge, the captain, the sergeant, the two privates, his executioners. They were in silhouette against the blue sky. They shouted and gesticulated, pointing at him. The captain had drawn his pistol, but did not fire; the others were unarmed. Their movements were grotesque and horrible, their forms gigantic.

Suddenly he heard a sharp report and something struck the water smartly within a few inches of his head, spattering his face with spray. He heard a second report, and saw one of the sentinels with his rifle at his shoulder, a light cloud of blue smoke rising from the muzzle. The man in the water saw the eye of the man on the bridge gazing into his own through the sights of the rifle. He observed that it was a gray eye and remembered having read that gray eyes were keenest, and that all famous marksmen had them. Nevertheless, this one had missed.

A counter-swirl had caught Farquhar and turned him half round; he was again looking at the forest on the bank opposite the fort. The sound of a clear, high voice in a monotonous singsong now rang out behind him and came across the water with a distinctness that pierced and subdued all other sounds, even the beating of the ripples in his ears. Although no soldier, he had frequented camps enough to know the dread significance of that deliberate, drawling, aspirated chant; the lieutenant on shore was taking a part in the morning's work. How coldly and pitilessly—with what an even, calm intonation, presaging, and enforcing tranquility in the men—with what accurately measured interval fell those cruel words:

"Company!... Attention!... Shoulder arms!... Ready!... Aim!... Fire!"

Farquhar dived—dived as deeply as he could. The water roared in his ears like the voice of Niagara, yet he heard the dull thunder of the volley and, rising again toward the surface, met shining bits of metal, singularly flattened, oscillating slowly downward. Some of them touched him on the face and hands, then fell away, continuing their descent. One lodged between his collar and neck; it was uncomfortably warm and he snatched it out.

As he rose to the surface, gasping for breath, he saw that he had been a long time under water; he was perceptibly farther downstream—nearer to safety. The soldiers had almost finished reloading; the metal ramrods flashed all at once in the sunshine as they were drawn from the barrels, turned in the air, and thrust into their sockets. The two sentinels fired again, independently and ineffectually.

The hunted man saw all this over his shoulder; he was now swimming vigorously with the current. His brain was as energetic as his arms and legs; he thought with the rapidity of lightning:

"The officer," he reasoned, "will not make that martinet's error a second time. It is as easy to dodge a volley as a single shot. He has probably already given the command to fire at will. God help me, I cannot dodge them all!"

An appalling splash within two yards of him was followed by a loud, rushing sound, DIMINUENDO, which seemed to travel back through the air to the fort and died in an explosion which stirred the very river to its deeps! A rising sheet of water curved over him, fell down upon him, blinded him, strangled him! The cannon had taken an hand in the game. As he shook his head free from the commotion of the smitten water he heard the deflected shot humming through the air ahead, and in an instant it was cracking and smashing the branches in the forest beyond.

"They will not do that again," he thought; "the next time they will use a charge of grape. I must keep my eye upon the gun; the smoke will apprise me—the report arrives too late; it lags behind the missile. That is a good gun."

Suddenly he felt himself whirled round and round—spinning like a top. The water, the banks, the forests, the now distant bridge, fort and men, all were commingled and blurred. Objects were represented by their colors only; circular horizontal streaks of color—that was all he saw. He had been caught in a vortex and was being whirled on with a velocity of advance and gyration that made him giddy and sick. In few moments he was flung upon the gravel at the foot of the left bank of the stream—the southern bank—and behind a projecting point which concealed him from his enemies. The sudden arrest of his motion, the abrasion of one of his hands on the gravel, restored him, and he wept with delight. He dug his fingers into the sand, threw it over himself in handfuls and audibly blessed it. It looked like diamonds, rubies, emeralds; he could think of nothing beautiful which it did not resemble. The trees upon the bank were giant garden plants; he noted a definite order in their arrangement, inhaled the fragrance of their blooms. A strange roseate light shone through the spaces among their trunks and the wind made in their branches the music of AEolian harps. He had not wish to perfect his escape—he was content to remain in that enchanting spot until retaken.

A whiz and a rattle of grapeshot among the branches high above his head roused him from his dream. The baffled cannoneer had fired him a random farewell. He sprang to his feet, rushed up the sloping bank, and plunged into the forest.

All that day he traveled, laying his course by the rounding sun. The forest seemed interminable; nowhere did he discover a break in it, not even a woodman's road. He had not known that he lived in so wild a region. There was something uncanny in the revelation.

By nightfall he was fatigued, footsore, famished. The thought of his wife and children urged him on. At last he found a road which led him in what he knew to be the right direction. It was as wide and straight as a city street, yet it seemed untraveled. No fields bordered it, no dwelling anywhere. Not so much as the barking of a dog suggested human habitation. The black bodies of the trees formed a straight wall on both sides, terminating on the horizon in a point, like a diagram in a lesson in perspective. Overhead, as he looked up through this rift in the wood, shone great golden stars looking unfamiliar and grouped in strange constellations. He was sure they were arranged in some order which had a secret and malign significance. The wood on either side was full of singular noises, among which—once, twice, and again—he distinctly heard whispers in an unknown tongue.

His neck was in pain and lifting his hand to it found it horribly swollen. He knew that it had a circle of black where the rope had bruised it. His eyes felt congested; he could no longer close them. His tongue was swollen with thirst; he relieved its fever by thrusting it forward from between his teeth into the cold air. How softly the turf had carpeted the untraveled avenue—he could no longer feel the roadway beneath his feet!

Doubtless, despite his suffering, he had fallen asleep while walking, for now he sees another scene—perhaps he has merely recovered from a delirium. He stands at the gate of his own home. All is as he left it, and all bright and beautiful in the morning sunshine. He must have traveled the entire night. As he pushes open the gate and passes up the wide white walk, he sees a flutter of female garments; his wife, looking fresh and cool and sweet, steps down from the veranda to meet him. At the bottom of the steps she stands waiting, with a smile of ineffable joy, an attitude of matchless grace and dignity. Ah, how beautiful she is! He springs forwards with extended arms. As he is about to clasp her he feels a stunning blow upon the back of the neck; a blinding white light blazes all about him with a sound like the shock of a cannon—then all is darkness and silence!

Peyton Farquhar was dead; his body, with a broken neck, swung gently from side to side beneath the timbers of the Owl Creek bridge.

Desiree's Baby
Kate Chopin

As the day was pleasant, Madame Valmonde drove over to L'Abri to see Desiree and the baby.

It made her laugh to think of Desiree with a baby. Why, it seemed but yesterday that Desiree was little more than a baby herself; when Monsieur in riding through the gateway of Valmonde had found her lying asleep in the shadow of the big stone pillar.

The little one awoke in his arms and began to cry for "Dada." That was as much as she could do or say. Some people thought she might have strayed there of her own accord, for she was of the toddling age. The prevailing belief was that she had been purposely left by a party of Texans, whose canvas-covered wagon, late in the day, had crossed the ferry that Coton Mais kept, just below the plantation. In time Madame Valmonde abandoned every speculation but the one that Desiree had been sent to her by a beneficent Providence to be the child of her affection, seeing that she was without child of the flesh. For the girl grew to be beautiful and gentle, affectionate and sincere,—the idol of Valmonde.

It was no wonder, when she stood one day against the stone pillar in whose shadow she had lain asleep, eighteen years before, that Armand Aubigny riding by and seeing her there, had fallen in love with her. That was the way all the Aubignys fell in love, as if struck by a pistol shot. The wonder was that he had not loved her before; for he had known her since his father brought him home from Paris, a boy of eight, after his mother died there. The passion that awoke in him that day, when he saw her at the gate, swept along like an avalanche, or like a prairie fire, or like anything that drives headlong over all obstacles.

Monsieur Valmonde grew practical and wanted things well considered: that is, the girl's obscure origin. Armand looked into her eyes and did not care. He was reminded that she was nameless. What did it matter about a name when he could give her one of the oldest and proudest in Louisiana? He ordered the corbeille from Paris, and contained himself with what patience he could until it arrived; then they were married.

Madame Valmonde had not seen Desiree and the baby for four weeks. When she reached L'Abri she shuddered at the first sight of it, as she always did. It was a sad looking place, which for many years had not known the gentle presence of a mistress, old Monsieur Aubigny having married and buried his wife in France, and she having loved her own land too well ever to leave it. The roof came down steep and black like a cowl, reaching out beyond the wide galleries that encircled the yellow stuccoed house. Big, solemn oaks grew close to it, and their thick-leaved, far-reaching branches shadowed it like a pall. Young Aubigny's rule was a strict one, too, and under it his negroes had forgotten how to be gay, as they had been during the old master's easy-going and indulgent lifetime.

The young mother was recovering slowly, and lay full length, in her soft white muslins and laces, upon a couch. The baby was beside her, upon her arm, where he had fallen asleep, at her breast. The yellow nurse woman sat beside a window fanning herself.

Madame Valmonde bent her portly figure over Desiree and kissed her, holding her an instant tenderly in her arms. Then she turned to the child.

"This is not the baby!" she exclaimed, in startled tones. French was the language spoken at Valmonde in those days.

"I knew you would be astonished," laughed Desiree, "at the way he has grown. The little cochon de lait! Look at his legs, mamma, and his hands and fingernails,—real finger-nails. Zandrine had to cut them this morning. Isn't it true, Zandrine?"

The woman bowed her turbaned head majestically, "Mais si, Madame."

"And the way he cries," went on Desiree, "is deafening. Armand heard him the other day as far away as La Blanche's cabin."

Madame Valmonde had never removed her eyes from the child. She lifted it and walked with it over to the window that was lightest. She scanned the baby narrowly, then looked as searchingly at Zandrine, whose face was turned to gaze across the fields.

"Yes, the child has grown, has changed," said Madame Valmonde, slowly, as she replaced it beside its mother. "What does Armand say?"

Desiree's face became suffused with a glow that was happiness itself.

"Oh, Armand is the proudest father in the parish, I believe, chiefly because it is a boy, to bear his name; though he says not,—that he would have loved a girl as well. But I know it isn't true. I know he says that to please me. And mamma," she added, drawing Madame Valmonde's head down to her, and speaking in a whisper, "he hasn't punished one of them—not one of them—since baby is born. Even Negrillon, who pretended to have burnt his leg that he might rest from work—he only laughed, and said Negrillon was a great scamp. Oh, mamma, I'm so happy; it frightens me."

What Desiree said was true. Marriage, and later the birth of his son had softened Armand Aubigny's imperious and exacting nature greatly. This was what made the gentle Desiree so happy, for she loved him desperately. When he frowned she trembled, but loved him. When he smiled, she asked no greater blessing of God. But Armand's dark, handsome face had not often been disfigured by frowns since the day he fell in love with her.

When the baby was about three months old, Desiree awoke one day to the conviction that there was something in the air menacing her peace. It was at first too subtle to grasp. It had only been a disquieting suggestion; an air of mystery among the blacks; unexpected visits from far-off neighbors who could hardly account for their coming. Then a strange, an awful change in her husband's manner, which she dared not ask him to explain. When he spoke to her, it was with averted eyes, from which the old love-light seemed to have gone out. He absented himself from home; and when there, avoided her presence and that of her child, without excuse. And the very spirit of Satan seemed suddenly to take hold of him in his dealings with the slaves. Desiree was miserable enough to die.

She sat in her room, one hot afternoon, in her peignoir, listlessly drawing through her fingers the strands of her long, silky brown hair that hung about her shoulders. The baby, half naked, lay asleep upon her own great mahogany bed, that was like a sumptuous throne, with its satin-lined half-canopy. One of La Blanche's little quadroon boys—half naked too—stood fanning the child slowly with a fan of peacock feathers. Desiree's eyes had been fixed absently and sadly upon the baby, while she was striving to penetrate the threatening mist that she felt closing about her. She looked from her child to the boy who stood beside him, and back again; over and over. "Ah!" It was a cry that she could not help; which she was not conscious of having uttered. The blood turned like ice in her veins, and a clammy moisture gathered upon her face.

She tried to speak to the little quadroon boy; but no sound would come, at first. When he heard his name uttered, he looked up, and his mistress was pointing to the door. He laid aside the great, soft fan, and obediently stole away, over the polished floor, on his bare tiptoes.

She stayed motionless, with gaze riveted upon her child, and her face the picture of fright.

Presently her husband entered the room, and without noticing her, went to a table and began to search among some papers which covered it.

"Armand," she called to him, in a voice which must have stabbed him, if he was human. But he did not notice. "Armand," she said again. Then she rose and tottered towards him. "Armand," she panted once more, clutching his arm, "look at our child. What does it mean? tell me."

He coldly but gently loosened her fingers from about his arm and thrust the hand away from him. "Tell me what it means!" she cried despairingly.

"It means," he answered lightly, "that the child is not white; it means that you are not white."

A quick conception of all that this accusation meant for her nerved her with unwonted courage to deny it. "It is a lie; it is not true, I am white! Look at my hair, it is brown; and my eyes are gray, Armand, you know they are gray. And my skin is fair," seizing his wrist. "Look at my hand; whiter than yours, Armand," she laughed hysterically.

"As white as La Blanche's," he returned cruelly; and went away leaving her alone with their child.

When she could hold a pen in her hand, she sent a despairing letter to Madame Valmonde.

"My mother, they tell me I am not white. Armand has told me I am not white. For God's sake tell them it is not true. You must know it is not true. I shall die. I must die. I cannot be so unhappy, and live."

The answer that came was brief:

"My own Desiree: Come home to Valmonde; back to your mother who loves you. Come with your child."

When the letter reached Desiree she went with it to her husband's study, and laid it open upon the desk before which he sat. She was like a stone image: silent, white, motionless after she placed it there.

In silence he ran his cold eyes over the written words.

He said nothing. "Shall I go, Armand?" she asked in tones sharp with agonized suspense.

"Yes, go."

"Do you want me to go?"

"Yes, I want you to go."

He thought Almighty God had dealt cruelly and unjustly with him; and felt, somehow, that he was paying Him back in kind when he stabbed thus into his wife's soul. Moreover he no longer loved her, because of the unconscious injury she had brought upon his home and his name.

She turned away like one stunned by a blow, and walked slowly towards the door, hoping he would call her back.

"Good-by, Armand," she moaned.

He did not answer her. That was his last blow at fate.

Desiree went in search of her child. Zandrine was pacing the sombre gallery with it. She took the little one from the nurse's arms with no word of explanation, and descending the steps, walked away, under the live-oak branches.

It was an October afternoon; the sun was just sinking. Out in the still fields the negroes were picking cotton.

Desiree had not changed the thin white garment nor the slippers which she wore. Her hair was uncovered and the sun's rays brought a golden gleam from its brown meshes. She did not take the broad, beaten road which led to the far-off plantation of Valmonde. She walked across a deserted field, where the stubble bruised her tender feet, so delicately shod, and tore her thin gown to shreds.

She disappeared among the reeds and willows that grew thick along the banks of the deep, sluggish bayou; and she did not come back again.

Some weeks later there was a curious scene enacted at L'Abri. In the centre of the smoothly swept back yard was a great bonfire. Armand Aubigny sat in the wide hallway that commanded a view of the spectacle; and it was he who dealt out to a half dozen negroes the material which kept this fire ablaze.

A graceful cradle of willow, with all its dainty furbishings, was laid upon the pyre, which had already been fed with the richness of a priceless layette. Then there were silk gowns, and velvet and satin ones added to

50

these; laces, too, and embroideries; bonnets and gloves; for the corbeille had been of rare quality.

The last thing to go was a tiny bundle of letters; innocent little scribblings that Desiree had sent to him during the days of their espousal. There was the remnant of one back in the drawer from which he took them. But it was not Desiree's; it was part of an old letter from his mother to his father. He read it. She was thanking God for the blessing of her husband's love:—

"But above all," she wrote, "night and day, I thank the good God for having so arranged our lives that our dear Armand will never know that his mother, who adores him, belongs to the race that is cursed with the brand of slavery."

Emily Dickinson

A Service of Song
Some keep the Sabbath going to church;
I keep it staying at home,
With a bobolink for a chorister,
And an orchard for a dome.
Some keep the Sabbath in surplice;
I just wear my wings,
And instead of tolling the bell for church,
Our little sexton sings.
God preaches, — a noted clergyman, —
And the sermon is never long;
So instead of getting to heaven at last,
I'm going all along!

The Chariot
Because I could not stop for Death,
He kindly stopped for me;
The carriage held but just ourselves
And Immortality.
We slowly drove, he knew no haste,
And I had put away
My labor, and my leisure too,
For his civility.
We passed the school where children played,
Their lessons scarcely done;
We passed the fields of gazing grain,
We passed the setting sun.
We paused before a house that seemed
A swelling of the ground;
The roof was scarcely visible,
The cornice but a mound.
Since then 't is centuries; but each
Feels shorter than the day
I first surmised the horses' heads
Were toward eternity.

Hope
Hope is the thing with feathers
That perches in the soul,
And sings the tune without the words,
And never stops at all,
And sweetest in the gale is heard;
And sore must be the storm

That could abash the little bird
That kept so many warm.
I 've heard it in the chillest land,
And on the strangest sea;
Yet, never, in extremity,
It asked a crumb of me.

By the Sea
I started early, took my dog,
And visited the sea;
The mermaids in the basement
Came out to look at me,
And frigates in the upper floor
Extended hempen hands,
Presuming me to be a mouse
Aground, upon the sands.
But no man moved me till the tide
Went past my simple shoe,
And past my apron and my belt,
And past my bodice too,
And made as he would eat me up
As wholly as a dew
Upon a dandelion's sleeve —
And then I started too.
And he — he followed close behind;
I felt his silver heel
Upon my ankle, — then my shoes
Would overflow with pearl.
Until we met the solid town,
No man he seemed to know;
And bowing with a mighty look
At me, the sea withdrew.

A Country Burial
Ample make this bed.
Make this bed with awe;
In it wait till judgment break
Excellent and fair.
Be its mattress straight,
Be its pillow round;
Let no sunrise' yellow noise
Interrupt this ground.

Griefs

53

I measure every grief I meet
  With analytic eyes;
I wonder if it weighs like mine,
  Or has an easier size.
I wonder if they bore it long,
  Or did it just begin?
I could not tell the date of mine,
  It feels so old a pain.
I wonder if it hurts to live,
  And if they have to try,
And whether, could they choose between,
  They would not rather die.
I wonder if when years have piled —
  Some thousands — on the cause
Of early hurt, if such a lapse
  Could give them any pause;
Or would they go on aching still
  Through centuries above,
Enlightened to a larger pain
  By contrast with the love.
The grieved are many, I am told;
  The reason deeper lies, —
Death is but one and comes but once,
  And only nails the eyes.
There's grief of want, and grief of cold, —
  A sort they call 'despair;'
There's banishment from native eyes,
  In sight of native air.
And though I may not guess the kind
  Correctly, yet to me
A piercing comfort it affords
  In passing Calvary,
To note the fashions of the cross,
  Of those that stand alone,
Still fascinated to presume
  That some are like my own.

Disenchantment

It dropped so low in my regard
  I heard it hit the ground,
And go to pieces on the stones
  At bottom of my mind;
Yet blamed the fate that fractured, less
  Than I reviled myself

For entertaining plated wares
Upon my silver shelf.

A.E. Housman

From *A Shropshire Lad*
III: The Recruit

Leave your home behind, lad,
And reach your friends your hand,
And go, and luck go with you
While Ludlow tower shall stand.

Oh, come you home of Sunday
When Ludlow streets are still
And Ludlow bells are calling
To farm and lane and mill,

Or come you home of Monday
When Ludlow market hums
And Ludlow chimes are playing
"The conquering hero comes,"

Come you home a hero,
Or come not home at all,
The lads you leave will mind you
Till Ludlow tower shall fall.

And you will list the bugle
That blows in lands of morn,
And make the foes of England
Be sorry you were born.

And you till trump of doomsday
On lands of morn may lie,
And make the hearts of comrades
Be heavy where you die.

Leave your home behind you,
Your friends by field and town
Oh, town and field will mind you
Till Ludlow tower is down.

IX

On moonlit heath and lonesome bank
The sheep beside me graze;
And yon the gallows used to clank
Fast by the four cross ways.

A careless shepherd once would keep
The flocks by moonlight there,
And high amongst the glimmering sheep
The dead man stood on air.

They hang us now in Shrewsbury jail:
The whistles blow forlorn,
And trains all night groan on the rail
To men that die at morn.

There sleeps in Shrewsbury jail to-night,
Or wakes, as may betide,
A better lad, if things went right,
Than most that sleep outside.

And naked to the hangman's noose
The morning clocks will ring
A neck God made for other use
Than strangling in a string.

And sharp the link of life will snap,
And dead on air will stand
Heels that held up as straight a chap
As treads upon the land.

So here I'll watch the night and wait
To see the morning shine,
When he will hear the stroke of eight
And not the stroke of nine;

And wish my friend as sound a sleep
As lads' I did not know,
That shepherded the moonlit sheep
A hundred years ago.

XIV

There pass the careless people
That call their souls their own:
Here by the road I loiter,
How idle and alone.

Ah, past the plunge of plummet,
In seas I cannot sound,
My heart and soul and senses,
World without end, are drowned.

57

His folly has not fellow
Beneath the blue of day
That gives to man or woman
His heart and soul away.

There flowers no balm to sain him
From east of earth to west
That's lost for everlasting
The heart out of his breast.

Here by the labouring highway
With empty hands I stroll:
Sea-deep, till doomsday morning,
Lie lost my heart and soul.

XV

Look not in my eyes, for fear
They mirror true the sight I see,
And there you find your face too clear
And love it and be lost like me.
One the long nights through must lie
Spent in star-defeated sighs,
But why should you as well as I
Perish? gaze not in my eyes.

A Grecian lad, as I hear tell,
One that many loved in vain,
Looked into a forest well
And never looked away again.
There, when the turf in springtime flowers,
With downward eye and gazes sad,
Stands amid the glancing showers
A jonquil, not a Grecian lad.

XVI

It nods and curtseys and recovers
When the wind blows above,
The nettle on the graves of lovers
That hanged themselves for love.

The nettle nods, the wind blows over,
The man, he does not move,
The lover of the grave, the lover
That hanged himself for love.

XIX: To an Athlete Dying Young

The time you won your town the race
We chaired you through the market-place;
Man and boy stood cheering by,
And home we brought you shoulder-high.

To-day, the road all runners come,
Shoulder-high we bring you home,
And set you at your threshold down,
Townsman of a stiller town.

Smart lad, to slip betimes away
From fields where glory does not stay
And early though the laurel grows
It withers quicker than the rose.

Eyes the shady night has shut
Cannot see the record cut,
And silence sounds no worse than cheers
After earth has stopped the ears:

Now you will not swell the rout
Of lads that wore their honours out,
Runners whom renown outran
And the name died before the man.

So set, before its echoes fade,
The fleet foot on the sill of shade,
And hold to the low lintel up
The still-defended challenge-cup.

And round that early-laurelled head
Will flock to gaze the strengthless dead,
And find unwithered on its curls
The garland briefer than a girl's.

XXII

The street sounds to the soldiers' tread,
And out we troop to see:
A single redcoat turns his head,
He turns and looks at me.

My man, from sky to sky's so far,
We never crossed before;

Such leagues apart the world's ends are,
We're like to meet no more;

What thoughts at heart have you and I
We cannot stop to tell;
But dead or living, drunk or dry,
Soldier, I wish you well.

XXVII

"Is my team ploughing,
That I was used to drive
And hear the harness jingle
When I was man alive?"

Ay, the horses trample,
The harness jingles now;
No change though you lie under
The land you used to plough.

"Is football playing
Along the river shore,
With lads to chase the leather,
Now I stand up no more?"

Ay, the ball is flying,
The lads play heart and soul;
The goal stands up, the keeper
Stands up to keep the goal.

"Is my girl happy,
That I thought hard to leave,
And has she tired of weeping
As she lies down at eve?"

Ay, she lies down lightly,
She lies not down to weep:
Your girl is well contented.
Be still, my lad, and sleep.

"Is my friend hearty,
Now I am thin and pine,
And has he found to sleep in
A better bed than mine?"

Yes, lad, I lie easy,

I lie as lads would choose;
I cheer a dead man's sweetheart,
Never ask me whose.

XXXIII

If truth in hearts that perish
Could move the powers on high,
I think the love I bear you
Should make you not to die.

Sure, sure, if stedfast meaning,
If single thought could save,
The world might end to-morrow,
You should not see the grave.

This long and sure-set liking,
This boundless will to please,
-Oh, you should live for ever
If there were help in these.

But now, since all is idle,
To this lost heart be kind,
Ere to a town you journey
Where friends are ill to find.

XXXVIII

The winds out of the west land blow,
My friends have breathed them there;
Warm with the blood of lads I know
Comes east the sighing air.

It fanned their temples, filled their lungs,
Scattered their forelocks free;
My friends made words of it with tongues
That talk no more to me.

Their voices, dying as they fly,
Thick on the wind are sown;
The names of men blow soundless by,
My fellows' and my own.

Oh lads, at home I heard you plain,
But here your speech is still,
And down the sighing wind in vain

You hollo from the hill.

The wind and I, we both were there,
But neither long abode;
Now through the friendless world we fare
And sigh upon the road.

XL

Into my heart an air that kills
From yon far country blows:
What are those blue remembered hills,
What spires, what farms are those?

That is the land of lost content,
I see it shining plain,
The happy highways where I went
And cannot come again.

XLIV

Shot? so quick, so clean an ending?
Oh that was right, lad, that was brave:
Yours was not an ill for mending,
'Twas best to take it to the grave.

Oh you had forethought, you could reason,
And saw your road and where it led,
And early wise and brave in season
Put the pistol to your head.

Oh soon, and better so than later
After long disgrace and scorn,
You shot dead the household traitor,
The soul that should not have been born.

Right you guessed the rising morrow
And scorned to tread the mire you must:
Dust's your wages, son of sorrow,
But men may come to worse than dust.

Souls undone, undoing others,-
Long time since the tale began.
You would not live to wrong your brothers:
Oh lad, you died as fits a man.

Now to your grave shall friend and stranger

With ruth and some with envy come:
Undishonoured, clear of danger,
Clean of guilt, pass hence and home.

Turn safe to rest, no dreams, no waking;
And here, man, here's the wreath I've made:
'Tis not a gift that's worth the taking,
But wear it and it will not fade.

XLV

If it chance your eye offend you,
Pluck it out, lad, and be sound:
'Twill hurt, but here are salves to friend you,
And many a balsam grows on ground.

And if your hand or foot offend you,
Cut it off, lad, and be whole;
But play the man, stand up and end you,
When your sickness is your soul.

LX

Now hollow fires burn out to black,
And lights are guttering low:
Square your shoulders, lift your pack,
And leave your friends and go.

Oh never fear, man, nought's to dread,
Look not left nor right:
In all the endless road you tread
There's nothing but the night.

LXIII

I Hoed and trenched and weeded,
And took the flowers to fair:
I brought them home unheeded;
The hue was not the wear.

So up and down I sow them
For lads like me to find,
When I shall lie below them,
A dead man out of mind.

Some seed the birds devour,
And some the season mars,
But here and there will flower

The solitary stars,

And fields will yearly bear them
As light-leaved spring comes on,
And luckless lads will wear them
When I am dead and gone.

From Last Poems
X
Could man be drunk for ever
With liquor, love, or fights,
Lief should I rouse at morning
And lief lie down of nights.

But men at whiles are sober
And think by fits and starts,
And if they think, they fasten
Their hands upon their hearts.

XI
Yonder see the morning blink:
The sun is up, and up must I,
To wash and dress and eat and drink
And look at things and talk and think
And work, and God knows why.

Oh often have I washed and dressed
And what's to show for all my pain?
Let me lie abed and rest:
Ten thousand times I've done my best
And all's to do again.

XII
The laws of God, the laws of man,
He may keep that will and can;
Now I: let God and man decree
Laws for themselves and not for me;
And if my ways are not as theirs
Let them mind their own affairs.
Their deeds I judge and much condemn,
Yet when did I make laws for them?
Please yourselves, say I, and they
Need only look the other way.
But no, they will not; they must still

Wrest their neighbour to their will,
And make me dance as they desire
With jail and gallows and hell-fire.
And how am I to face the odds
Of man's bedevilment and God's?
I, a stranger and afraid
In a world I never made.
They will be master, right or wrong;
Though both are foolish, both are strong,
And since, my soul, we cannot fly
To Saturn or Mercury,
Keep we must, if keep we can,
These foreign laws of God and man.

XIV
The Culprit
The night my father got me
　His mind was not on me;
He did not plague his fancy
　To muse if I should be
　The son you see.

The day my mother bore me
　She was a fool and glad,
For all the pain I cost her,
　That she had borne the lad
　That borne she had.

My mother and my father
　Out of the light they lie;
The warrant would not find them,
　And here 'tis only I
　Shall hang so high.

Oh let not man remember
　The soul that God forgot,
But fetch the county kerchief
　And noose me in the knot,
　And I will rot.

For so the game is ended
　That should not have begun.
My father and my mother
　They had a likely son,
　And I have none.

XV: Eight O'Clock

He stood, and heard the steeple
 Sprinkle the quarters on the morning town.
One, two, three, four, to market-place and people
 It tossed them down.

Strapped, noosed, nighing his hour,
 He stood and counted them and cursed his luck;
And then the clock collected in the tower
 Its strength, and struck.

XXXII

When I would muse in boyhood
 The wild green woods among,
And nurse resolves and fancies
 Because the world was young,
It was not foes to conquer,
 Nor sweethearts to be kind,
But it was friends to die for
 That I would seek and find.

I sought them far and found them,
 The sure, the straight, the brave,
The hearts I lost my own to,
 The souls I could not save.
They braced their belts about them,
 They crossed in ships the sea,
They sought and found six feet of ground,
 And there they died for me.

From *More Poems*
XXX

Shake hands, we shall never be friends, all's over;
 I only vex you the more I try.
All's wrong that ever I've done or said,
And nought to help it in this dull head:
 Shake hands, here's luck, good-bye.

But if you come to a road where danger
 Or guilt or anguish or shame's to share,
Be good to the lad that loves you true
And the soul that was born to die for you,
 And whistle and I'll be there.

XXXI

Because I liked you better
  Than suits a man to say,
It irked you, and I promised
  To throw the thought away.

To put the world between us
  We parted, stiff and dry;
`Good-bye,' said you, `forget me.'
  `I will, no fear', said I.

If here, where clover whitens
  The dead man's knoll, you pass,
And no tall flower to meet you
  Starts in the trefoiled grass,

Halt by the headstone naming
  The heart no longer stirred,
And say the lad that loved you
  Was one that kept his word.

XLII – A.J.J.

When he's returned I'll tell him – oh,
  Dear fellow, I forgot:
Time was you would have cared to know,
  But now it matters not.

I mourn you, and you heed not how;
  Unsaid the word must stay;
Last month was time enough, but now
  The news must keep for aye.

Oh, many a month before I learn
  Will find me starting still
And listening, as the days return,
  For him that never will.

Strange, strange to think his blood is cold
  And mine flows easy on:
And that straight look, that heart of gold,
  That grace, that manhood gone.

The word unsaid will stay unsaid
  Though there was much to say;
Last month was time enough: he's dead,

The news must keep for aye.

From *Additional Poems*
IV
It is no gift I tender,
 A loan is all I can;
But do not scorn the lender;
 Man gets no more from man.

Oh, mortal man may borrow
 What mortal man can lend;
And 'twill not end to-morrow,
 Though sure enough 'twill end.

If death and time are stronger,
 A love may yet be strong;
The world will last for longer,
 But this will last for long.

XVIII: Oh Who Is That Young Sinner
 Oh who is that young sinner with the handcuffs on his wrists?
And what has he been after that they groan and shake their fists?
And wherefore is he wearing such a conscience-stricken air?
Oh they're taking him to prison for the colour of his hair.

'Tis a shame to human nature, such a head of hair as his;
In the good old time 'twas hanging for the colour that it is;
Though hanging isn't bad enough and flaying would be fair
For the nameless and abominable colour of his hair.

Oh a deal of pains he's taken and a pretty price he's paid
To hide his poll or dye it of a mentionable shade;
But they've pulled the beggar's hat off for the world to see and stare,
And they're haling him to justice for the colour of his hair.

Now 'tis oakum for his fingers and the treadmill for his feet
And the quarry-gang on Portland in the cold and in the heat,
And between his spells of labour in the time he has to spare
He can curse the God that made him for the colour of his hair.

Siegfried Sassoon

Dreamers

Soldiers are citizens of death's grey land,
  Drawing no dividend from time's to-morrows.
In the great hour of destiny they stand,
  Each with his feuds, and jealousies, and sorrows.
Soldiers are sworn to action; they must win
  Some flaming, fatal climax with their lives.
Soldiers are dreamers; when the guns begin
  They think of firelit homes, clean beds, and wives.
I see them in foul dug-outs, gnawed by rats,
  And in the ruined trenches, lashed with rain,
Dreaming of things they did with balls and bats,
  And mocked by hopeless longing to regain
Bank-holidays, and picture shows, and spats,
  And going to the office in the train.

The Hero

"Jack fell as he'd have wished," the Mother said,
And folded up the letter that she'd read.
"The Colonel writes so nicely." Something broke
In the tired voice that quavered to a choke.
She half looked up. "We mothers are so proud
Of our dead soldiers." Then her face was bowed.
Quietly the Brother Officer went out.
He'd told the poor old dear some gallant lies
That she would nourish all her days, no doubt.
For while he coughed and mumbled, her weak eyes
Had shone with gentle triumph, brimmed with joy,
Because he'd been so brave, her glorious boy.
He thought how "Jack," cold-footed, useless swine,
Had panicked down the trench that night the mine
Went up at Wicked Corner; how he'd tried
To get sent home; and how, at last, he died,
Blown to small bits. And no one seemed to care
Except that lonely woman with white hair.

The Dug-Out

Why do you lie with your legs ungainly huddled,
And one arm bent across your sullen cold
Exhausted face? It hurts my heart to watch you,
Deep-shadow'd from the candle's guttering gold;
And you wonder why I shake you by the shoulder;
Drowsy, you mumble and sigh and turn your head....

69

You are too young to fall asleep for ever;
And when you sleep you remind me of the dead.

"They"

The Bishop tells us: "When the boys come back
They will not be the same; for they'll have fought
In a just cause: they lead the last attack
On Anti-Christ; their comrade's blood has bought
New right to breed an honourable race.
They have challenged Death and dared him face to face."
"We're none of us the same!" the boys reply.
"For George lost both his legs; and Bill's stone blind;
Poor Jim's shot through the lungs and like to die;
And Bert's gone syphilitic: you'll not find
A chap who's served that hasn't found *some* change."
And the Bishop said; "The ways of God are strange!"

How to Die

Dark clouds are smouldering into red
  While down the craters morning burns.
The dying soldier shifts his head
  To watch the glory that returns:
He lifts his fingers toward the skies
  Where holy brightness breaks in flame;
Radiance reflected in his eyes,
  And on his lips a whispered name.
You'd think, to hear some people talk,
  That lads go West with sobs and curses,
And sullen faces white as chalk,
  Hankering for wreaths and tombs and hearses.
But they've been taught the way to do it
  Like Christian soldiers; not with haste
And shuddering groans; but passing through it
  With due regard for decent taste.

Sick Leave

When I'm asleep, dreaming and lulled and warm,—
They come, the homeless ones, the noiseless dead.
While the dim charging breakers of the storm
Bellow and drone and rumble overhead,
Out of the gloom they gather about my bed.
They whisper to my heart; their thoughts are mine.
"Why are you here with all your watches ended?
From Ypres to Frise we sought you in the Line."
In bitter safety I awake, unfriended;

70

And while the dawn begins with slashing rain
I think of the Battalion in the mud.
"When are you going out to them again?
Are they not still your brothers through our blood?"

Banishment

I am banished from the patient men who fight.
They smote my heart to pity, built my pride.
Shoulder to aching shoulder, side by side,
They trudged away from life's broad wealds of light.
Their wrongs were mine; and ever in my sight
They went arrayed in honour. But they died,—
Not one by one: and mutinous I cried
To those who sent them out into the night.
The darkness tells how vainly I have striven
To free them from the pit where they must dwell
In outcast gloom convulsed and jagged and riven
By grappling guns. Love drove me to rebel.
Love drives me back to grope with them through hell;
And in their tortured eyes I stand forgiven.

Together

Splashing along the boggy woods all day,
And over brambled hedge and holding clay,
I shall not think of him:
But when the watery fields grow brown and dim,
And hounds have lost their fox, and horses tire,
I know that he'll be with me on my way
Home through the darkness to the evening fire.
He's jumped each stile along the glistening lanes;
His hand will be upon the mud-soaked reins;
Hearing the saddle creak,
He'll wonder if the frost will come next week.
I shall forget him in the morning light;
And while we gallop on he will not speak:
But at the stable-door he'll say good-night.

A Letter Home

(To Robert Graves)

I

Here I'm sitting in the gloom
Of my quiet attic room.
France goes rolling all around,
Fledged with forest May has crowned.
And I puff my pipe, calm-hearted,

71

Thinking how the fighting started,
Wondering when we'll ever end it,
Back to Hell with Kaiser send it,
Gag the noise, pack up and go,
Clockwork soldiers in a row.
I've got better things to do
Than to waste my time on you.

II
Robert, when I drowse to-night,
Skirting lawns of sleep to chase
Shifting dreams in mazy light,
Somewhere then I'll see your face
Turning back to bid me follow
Where I wag my arms and hollo,
Over hedges hasting after
Crooked smile and baffling laughter,
Running tireless, floating, leaping,
Down your web-hung woods and valleys,
Garden glooms and hornbeam alleys,
Where the glowworm stars are peeping,
Till I find you, quiet as stone
On a hill-top all alone,
Staring outward, gravely pondering
Jumbled leagues of hillock-wandering.

III
You and I have walked together
In the starving winter weather.
We've been glad because we knew
Time's too short and friends are few.
We've been sad because we missed
One whose yellow head was kissed
By the gods, who thought about him
Till they couldn't do without him.
Now he's here again; I've seen
Soldier David dressed in green,
Standing in a wood that swings
To the madrigal he sings.
He's come back, all mirth and glory,
Like the prince in a fairy story.
Winter called him far away;
Blossoms bring him home with May.

72

IV

Well, I know you'll swear it's true
That you found him decked in blue
Striding up through morning-land
With a cloud on either hand.
Out in Wales, you'll say, he marches
Arm-in-arm with oaks and larches;
Hides all night in hilly nooks,
Laughs at dawn in tumbling brooks.
Yet, it's certain, here he teaches
Outpost-schemes to groups of beeches.
And I'm sure, as here I stand,
That he shines through every land,
That he sings in every place
Where we're thinking of his face.

V

Robert, there's a war in France;
Everywhere men bang and blunder,
Sweat and swear and worship Chance,
Creep and blink through cannon thunder.
Rifles crack and bullets flick,
Sing and hum like hornet-swarms.
Bones are smashed and buried quick.
Yet, through stunning battle storms,
All the while I watch the spark
Lit to guide me; for I know
Dreams will triumph, though the dark
Scowls above me where I go.
You can hear me; *you* can mingle
Radiant folly with my jingle,
War's a joke for me and you
While we know such dreams are true!

Aftermath

Have you forgotten yet?...
> For the world's events have rumbled on since those gagged days,
> Like traffic checked awhile at the crossing of city ways:
> And the haunted gap in your mind has filled with thoughts that flow
> Like clouds in the lit heavens of life; and you're a man reprieved to go,
> Taking your peaceful share of Time, with joy to spare.
> *But the past is just the same,—and War's a bloody game,...*
> *Have you forgotten yet?...*
> *Look down, and swear by the slain of the War that you'll never forget.*

Do you remember the dark months you held the sector at Mametz,—
The nights you watched and wired and dug and piled sandbags on
parapets?
Do you remember the rats; and the stench
Of corpses rotting in front of the front-line trench,—
And dawn coming, dirty-white, and chill with a hopeless rain?
Do you ever stop and ask, "Is it all going to happen again?"
Do you remember that hour of din before the attack,—
And the anger, the blind compassion that seized and shook you then
As you peered at the doomed and haggard faces of your men?
Do you remember the stretcher-cases lurching back
With dying eyes and lolling heads,—those ashen-grey
Masks of the lads who once were keen and kind and gay?
Have you forgotten yet?... Look up, and swear by the green of the Spring that you'll
never forget.

Wilfred Owen

Maundy Thursday

Between the brown hands of a server-lad
The silver cross was offered to be kissed.
The men came up, lugubrious, but not sad,
And knelt reluctantly, half-prejudiced.
(And kissing, kissed the emblem of a creed.)
Then mourning women knelt; meek mouths they had,
(And kissed the Body of the Christ indeed.)
Young children came, with eager lips and glad.
(These kissed a silver doll, immensely bright.)
Then I, too, knelt before that acolyte.
Above the crucifix I bent my head:
The Christ was thin, and cold, and very dead:
And yet I bowed, yea, kissed - my lips did cling.
(I kissed the warm live hand that held the thing.)

Greater Love

Red lips are not so red
As the stained stones kissed by the English dead.
Kindness of wooed and wooer
Seems shame to their love pure.
O Love, your eyes lose lure
When I behold eyes blinded in my stead!

Your slender attitude
Trembles not exquisite like limbs knife-skewed,
Rolling and rolling there
Where God seems not to care;
Till the fierce Love they bear
Cramps them in death's extreme decrepitude.

Your voice sings not so soft,—
Though even as wind murmuring through raftered loft,—
Your dear voice is not dear,
Gentle, and evening clear,
As theirs whom none now hear
Now earth has stopped their piteous mouths that coughed.

Heart, you were never hot,
Nor large, nor full like hearts made great with shot;
And though your hand be pale,
Paler are all which trail
Your cross through flame and hail:

Weep, you may weep, for you may touch them not.

Apologia pro Poemate Meo

I, too, saw God through mud—
  The mud that cracked on cheeks when wretches smiled.
War brought more glory to their eyes than blood,
  And gave their laughs more glee than shakes a child.

Merry it was to laugh there—
  Where death becomes absurd and life absurder.
For power was on us as we slashed bones bare
  Not to feel sickness or remorse of murder.

I, too, have dropped off fear—
  Behind the barrage, dead as my platoon,
And sailed my spirit surging, light and clear
  Past the entanglement where hopes lay strewn;

And witnessed exultation—
  Faces that used to curse me, scowl for scowl,
Shine and lift up with passion of oblation,
  Seraphic for an hour; though they were foul.

I have made fellowships—
  Untold of happy lovers in old song.
For love is not the binding of fair lips
  With the soft silk of eyes that look and long,

By Joy, whose ribbon slips,—
  But wound with war's hard wire whose stakes are strong;
Bound with the bandage of the arm that drips;
  Knit in the welding of the rifle-thong.

I have perceived much beauty
  In the hoarse oaths that kept our courage straight;
Heard music in the silentness of duty;
  Found peace where shell-storms spouted reddest spate.

Nevertheless, except you share
  With them in hell the sorrowful dark of hell,
Whose world is but the trembling of a flare,
  And heaven but as the highway for a shell,

You shall not hear their mirth:
  You shall not come to think them well content

By any jest of mine. These men are worth
Your tears: You are not worth their merriment.

Parable of the Old Men and the Young

So Abram rose, and clave the wood, and went,
And took the fire with him, and a knife.
And as they sojourned both of them together,
Isaac the first-born spake and said, My Father,
Behold the preparations, fire and iron,
But where the lamb for this burnt-offering?
Then Abram bound the youth with belts and straps,
And builded parapets and trenches there,
And stretched forth the knife to slay his son.
When lo! an angel called him out of heaven,
Saying, Lay not thy hand upon the lad,
Neither do anything to him. Behold,
A ram caught in a thicket by its horns;
Offer the Ram of Pride instead of him.
But the old man would not so, but slew his son,
And half the seed of Europe, one by one.

Arms and the Boy

Let the boy try along this bayonet-blade
How cold steel is, and keen with hunger of blood;
Blue with all malice, like a madman's flash;
And thinly drawn with famishing for flesh.

Lend him to stroke these blind, blunt bullet-heads
Which long to muzzle in the hearts of lads.
Or give him cartridges of fine zinc teeth,
Sharp with the sharpness of grief and death.

For his teeth seem for laughing round an apple.
There lurk no claws behind his fingers supple;
And God will grow no talons at his heels,
Nor antlers through the thickness of his curls.

Anthem for Doomed Youth

What passing-bells for these who die as cattle?
Only the monstrous anger of the guns.
Only the stuttering rifles' rapid rattle
Can patter out their hasty orisons.
No mockeries for them; no prayers nor bells,
Nor any voice of mourning save the choirs,—
The shrill, demented choirs of wailing shells;

And bugles calling for them from sad shires.

What candles may be held to speed them all?
Not in the hands of boys, but in their eyes
Shall shine the holy glimmers of goodbyes.
The pallor of girls' brows shall be their pall;
Their flowers the tenderness of patient minds,
And each slow dusk a drawing-down of blinds.

Dulce et Decorum est

Bent double, like old beggars under sacks,
Knock-kneed, coughing like hags, we cursed through sludge,
Till on the haunting flares we turned our backs,
And towards our distant rest began to trudge.
Men marched asleep. Many had lost their boots,
But limped on, blood-shod. All went lame, all blind;
Drunk with fatigue; deaf even to the hoots
Of gas-shells dropping softly behind.

Gas! GAS! Quick, boys!—An ecstasy of fumbling
Fitting the clumsy helmets just in time,
But someone still was yelling out and stumbling
And flound'ring like a man in fire or lime.—
Dim through the misty panes and thick green light,
As under a green sea, I saw him drowning.

In all my dreams before my helpless sight
He plunges at me, guttering, choking, drowning.

If in some smothering dreams, you too could pace
Behind the wagon that we flung him in,
And watch the white eyes writhing in his face,
His hanging face, like a devil's sick of sin,
If you could hear, at every jolt, the blood
Come gargling from the froth-corrupted lungs
Bitter as the cud
Of vile, incurable sores on innocent tongues,—
My friend, you would not tell with such high zest
To children ardent for some desperate glory,
The old Lie: *Dulce et decorum est*
Pro patria mori.

Futility

Move him into the sun—
Gently its touch awoke him once,

78

At home, whispering of fields unsown.
Always it woke him, even in France,
Until this morning and this snow.
If anything might rouse him now
The kind old sun will know.

Think how it wakes the seeds—
Woke, once, the clays of a cold star.
Are limbs so dear-achieved, are sides
Full-nerved,—still warm,—too hard to stir?
Was it for this the clay grew tall?
—O what made fatuous sunbeams toil
To break earth's sleep at all?

W. B. Yeats

The Lake Isle of Innisfree
I will arise and go now, and go to Innisfree,
And a small cabin build there, of clay and wattles made:
Nine bean rows will I have there, a hive for the honey bee,
And live alone in the bee-loud glade.

And I shall have some peace there, for peace comes dropping slow,
Dropping from the veils of the morning to where the cricket sings;
There midnight's all a glimmer, and noon a purple glow,
And evening full of the linnet's wings.

I will arise and go now, for always night and day
I hear lake water lapping with low sounds by the shore;
While I stand on the roadway, or on the pavements gray,
I hear it in the deep heart's core.

When You Are Old
When you are old and gray and full of sleep,
And nodding by the fire, take down this book,
And slowly read, and dream of the soft look
Your eyes had once, and of their shadows deep;

How many loved your moments of glad grace,
And loved your beauty will love false or true;
But one man loved the pilgrim soul in you,
And loved the sorrows of your changing face.

And bending down beside the glowing bars
Murmur, a little sadly, how love fled
And paced upon the mountains overhead
And hid his face amid a crowd of stars.

The Stolen Child
Where dips the rocky highland
Of Sleuth Wood in the lake,
There lies a leafy island
Where flapping herons wake
The drowsy water rats;
There we've hid our faery vats,
Full of berries,
And of reddest stolen cherries.
Come away, O human child!
To the waters and the wild

With a faery, hand in hand,
For the world's more full of weeping than you can understand.

Where the wave of moonlight glosses
The dim gray sands with light,
Far off by furthest Rosses
We foot it all the night,
Weaving olden dances,
Mingling hands and mingling glances
Till the moon has taken flight;
To and fro we leap
And chase the frothy bubbles,
While the world is full of troubles
And is anxious in its sleep.
Come away, O human child!
To the waters and the wild
With a faery, hand in hand,
For the world's more full of weeping than you can understand.

Where the wandering water gushes
From the hills above Glen-Car,
In pools among the rushes
That scarce could bathe a star,
We seek for slumbering trout
And whispering in their ears
Give them unquiet dreams;
Leaning softly out
From ferns that drop their tears
Over the young streams,
Come away, O human child!
To the waters and the wild
With a faery, hand in hand,
For the world's more full of weeping than you can understand.

Away with us he's going,
The solemn-eyed:
He'll hear no more the lowing
Of the calves on the warm hillside
Or the kettle on the hob
Sing peace into his breast,
Or see the brown mice bob
Round and round the oatmeal-chest.
For he comes, the human child,
To the waters and the wild

With a faery, hand in hand,
From a world more full of weeping than he can understand.

No Second Troy

Why should I blame her that she filled my days
With misery, or that she would of late
Have taught to ignorant men most violent ways,
Or hurled the little streets upon the great,
Had they but courage equal to desire?
What could have made her peaceful with a mind
That nobleness made simple as a fire,
With beauty like a tightened bow, a kind
That is not natural in an age like this,
Being high and solitary and most stern?
Why, what could she have done being what she is?
Was there another Troy for her to burn?

An Irish Airman Foresees His Death

I know that I shall meet my fate
Somewhere among the clouds above;
Those that I fight I do not hate
Those that I guard I do not love;
My country is Kiltartan Cross,
My countrymen Kiltartan's poor,
No likely end could bring them loss
Or leave them happier than before.
Nor law, nor duty bade me fight,
Nor public man, nor angry crowds,
A lonely impulse of delight
Drove to this tumult in the clouds;
I balanced all, brought all to mind,
The years to come seemed waste of breath,
A waste of breath the years behind
In balance with this life, this death.

The Second Coming

Turning and turning in the widening gyre
The falcon cannot hear the falconer;
Things fall apart; the centre cannot hold;
Mere anarchy is loosed upon the world,
The blood-dimmed tide is loosed, and everywhere
The ceremony of innocence is drowned;
The best lack all conviction, while the worst
Are full of passionate intensity.

Surely some revelation is at hand;
Surely the Second Coming is at hand.
The Second Coming! Hardly are those words out
When a vast image out of Spiritus Mundi
Troubles my sight: somewhere in sands of the desert
A shape with lion body and the head of a man,
A gaze blank and pitiless as the sun,
Is moving its slow thighs, while all about it
Reel shadows of the indignant desert birds.
The darkness drops again; but now I know
That twenty centuries of stony sleep
Were vexed to nightmare by a rocking cradle,
And what rough beast, its hour come round at last,
Slouches towards Bethlehem to be born?

Edna St. Vincent Millay

Witch-Wife
She is neither pink nor pale,
And she never will be all mine;
She learned her hands in a fairy-tale,
And her mouth on a valentine.
She has more hair than she needs;
In the sun 'tis a woe to me!
And her voice is a string of colored beads,
Or steps leading into the sea.
She loves me all that she can,
And her ways to my ways resign;
But she was not made for any man,
And she never will be all mine.

Dirge
Boys and girls that held her dear,
 Do your weeping now;
All you loved of her lies here.

Brought to earth the arrogant brow,
 And the withering tongue
Chastened; do your weeping now.

Sing whatever songs are sung,
 Wind whatever wreath,
For a playmate perished young,

For a spirit spent in death.
Boys and girls that held her dear,
All you loved of her lies here.

Sonnet IV
I shall forget you presently, my dear,
 So make the most of this, your little day,
 Your little month, your little half a year,
 Ere I forget, or die, or move away,
 And we are done forever; by and by
 I shall forget you, as I said, but now,
 If you entreat me with your loveliest lie
 I will protest you with my favorite vow.
 I would indeed that love were longer-lived,
 And oaths were not so brittle as they are,
 But so it is, and nature has contrived

To struggle on without a break thus far,—
Whether or not we find what we are seeking
Is idle, biologically speaking.

Sonnet V

What lips my lips have kissed, and where, and why,
I have forgotten, and what arms have lain
Under my head till morning; but the rain
Is full of ghosts to-night, that tap and sigh
Upon the glass and listen for reply;
And in my heart there stirs a quiet pain,
For unremembered lads that not again
Will turn to me at midnight with a cry.
Thus in the winter stands the lonely tree,
Nor knows what birds have vanished one by one,
Yet knows its boughs more silent than before:
I cannot say what loves have come and gone;
I only know that summer sang in me
A little while, that in me sings no more.

Robert Frost

The Road Not Taken

Two roads diverged in a yellow wood,
And sorry I could not travel both
And be one traveler, long I stood
And looked down one as far as I could
To where it bent in the undergrowth;

Then took the other, as just as fair,
And having perhaps the better claim,
Because it was grassy and wanted wear;
Though as for that the passing there
Had worn them really about the same,

And both that morning equally lay
In leaves no step had trodden black.
Oh, I kept the first for another day!
Yet knowing how way leads on to way,
I doubted if I should ever come back.

I shall be telling this with a sigh
Somewhere ages and ages hence:
Two roads diverged in a wood, and I—
I took the one less traveled by,
And that has made all the difference.

Fire and Ice

Some say the world will end in fire,
Some say in ice.
From what I've tasted of desire
I hold with those who favor fire.
But if it had to perish twice,
I think I know enough of hate
To know that for destruction ice
Is also great,
And would suffice.

Writing Personal Narratives

When we write about ourselves, we construct an image of ourselves that we present to the world. What we present depends on the circumstances: to whom we are writing--that is, our audience--and why we are writing the essay to begin with--our purpose. It is our audience and our purpose that will determine what we want to say, how we say it, and how much we decide to reveal about ourselves.

Leon Uris, in his novel *Trinity*, talks about the "rooms" we all have inside ourselves. Uris says we have:

- A large outer room: our public persona; the face we show the world.

- A small outer room: our private persona; what we reveal to our family and friends.

- A large inner room: our private thoughts; the things we know about ourselves but keep secret from everyone.

- And a small inner room: our subconscious; the things that scare us so much that we don't allow even ourselves to think about them.

Clearly, when you write this type of paper, you will need to be cautious about entering these inner rooms for your material. There are some things you wouldn't want to reveal, and it probably wouldn't be appropriate for you to reveal them. On the other hand, you don't want to deal only with the superficial. You don't want your paper to sound "shallow." For a remembered event essay to work, it must have substance. Thus, in most cases, you will want to write inside that small outer room and treat your reader as a friend. There's a line from a song by a band called T. Rex that goes, "Book after book, I get hooked every time the writer talks to me like a friend." This is true for most of us. As readers, we don't want to be treated as an outsider. So, as writers, we don't want to seem aloof from our readers. Your readers may not be able to identify with everything you write about, but they will respect an honest voice; good writers strive for honesty in their self-disclosure.

Before you begin to write, even before you select your topic, you need to think about the important features of this type of essay: (1) a well-told story, (2) a vivid presentation of scenes and people, and (3) an indication of significance.

A Well-told Story

Whatever you write about, you must present the material in a way that makes the readers want to keep reading. Shape the experience in a way that is both entertaining and memorable. Create suspense. Your readers may be shuddering because they sense impending disaster or an unpleasant disclosure, or they may be grinning because they anticipate a humorous turn of events. The important thing is that they want to know what will happen. **How you tell the story is far more important than the story being told.** Maybe nothing exciting has ever happened to you.

You can still pick some quirky event in your life and relate the experience in a way that entertains people. On the other hand, your life may have been filled with trips to Africa and the Pacific, climbing mountains, and surviving avalanches, but if your story is poorly-written, nobody will want to read it.

Sequencing. Think about the sequence of actions that took place and how you want to present them. Usually, a chronological presentation works best--that is, you start at the beginning and narrate the action until you get to the end. But there are times when flashbacks and beginning *in medias res* (in the midst of things) work well. You might even present the climax of your story first and then relate the events leading up to it. Or you might begin at the point just prior to the climax, then flash back to the beginning and end your story with the climax.

You also need to think about **conflict.** This is usually some struggle between the main character and an opposing force, such as another person or animal, nature or society. But the conflict may also be internal-- a character at war with himself. Conflict gives purpose to the action of the story. Instead of straight chronology (this happened then this happened then this happened, conflict provides a one-thing-leads-to another structure. The conflict is what presents the **tensions** in the story that make readers want to keep reading. You use conflict to stretch the narrative line of your story, and this stretching, just like on a tennis racquet, creates the tension: readers are strung along because they care about the ultimate resolution of the conflict. They look forward to the **climax**, which is the point when tension is highest and when the outcome is determined.

Early on in Thomas Woolf's short story "The Lost Boy," Woolf writes about his title character: "Out of the tension of those quiet eyes some brightness had gone, and into their vision had come some deeper color. He could not say, he did not know, through what transforming shadows life had passed within that quarter hour. He only knew that something had been lost--something forever gained."

This passage creates tension because we as readers want to know what has been lost,
what forever gained. In short, we want to what on earth he's talking about and why there's this air of mystery around it. To find out, we keep reading.

Tension is also created by **pace.** As a writer, you pace your story by emphasizing certain things over others. If you give equal emphasis to everything, your story becomes monotonous. But if, when you come to an important part of your story, you change the pace, this creates tension. You can slow down the action with dialogue and detailed descriptions. You can speed up the action by choosing vivid verbs and using less description.

Usually, you will want to vary the length of your sentences to create rhythm. Here is an example from Russell Baker: "The wheels were hardly off the mat before I experienced another eerie sensation. It was a feeling of power. For the first time since first stepping into an airplane, I felt in complete mastery of the thing. I'd noticed it on takeoff. It had been an excellent takeoff. Without thinking about it, I'd automatically corrected a slight swerve just before becoming airborne."

Notice the length of each sentence: long sentence, short sentence, long, short, long. This is good variety. If you use all long sentences, you wear your readers out. You must give them chances to breathe. But, except in special situations when you're trying to make a point, if you use all short sentences, it has the same effect on your reader. All the stopping and starting wears them out, like driving through a city in which you get caught at a red light on every corner and you have to stop just as you are starting to get going. And just as only short sentences is like driving stop-start through town, the tedium of nothing but long sentences is like driving through western Kansas. Just as the driver is thinking, "Will I ever get to the end of this road?" your reader may be thinking, "Will I ever get to the end of this sentence?" You should alter the length of your sentences to create variety and rhythm.

Dialogue is another important element in your story. You use dialogue to reveal your conflict directly, without having to intrude yourself. When dialogue is effective, readers gain insights into the personality and motives of the characters--and readers are placed in the middle of the story, with it unfolding right before their eyes. You can use dialogue to show characters being afraid, or defensive, or obnoxious, or funny, or courageous, or honest, or deceptive-- anything you can say about a character, you can also have that character reveal himself through his own words or actions.

Rather than just telling us a person is kind, put that character in a scene in which his actions will show us that his kind. Show the readers how the characters behave, don't just tell them. Then remember how the character talked and give him some dialogue. When we hear characters talking, we can infer from their own words what they are like, how they think, and how they feel about one another. It's much more effective. This is how characters come alive for the reader.

In using dialogue effectively, you must have an ear for what each character sounds like. Most people have very different speech patterns from each other, and your dialogue should reflect this. You don't want all of your characters sounding the same.

A Vivid Presentation of Significant Scenes and People

Scenes and people play important roles in remembered event essays. A good writer will re-create the scenes and allow us to feel like we know the people by giving us vivid, specific descriptions: carefully selected details that allow us to hear, feel, see, and even smell and taste what is going on as the story unfolds.

The mere act of **naming** specific objects helps. You think about the scene you're writing about and recall from your own memory what made an impression on you: a tie clasp, rain, a dress. Then you provide some details about the objects through description: a gold tie clasp, a stinging rain, a red and white checkered tent dress. Finally, you can use simile and metaphor to make comparisons: a gold tie clasp shaped like the state of Texas, a stinging rain hitting her face like bullets, a red-and-white-checkered tent dress that looked like a Purina dog food sack.

When you name things, sometime it can be useful to name them by brand. Instead of a car, say a Chevy; instead of a soft drink, say a Dr. Pepper. Don't do this too often, because it would become distracting and lose its effectiveness, but every once in a while, you might want to throw one in. If you do, it's best to pick something that everyone knows and that is likely to be around for a while, especially if you're writing something that you hope will be read for years to come.

Just as specific brand names can make something more vivid, so does providing good details or descriptions. When you start describing the things you've named, you'll be using modifiers-- adjectives, adverbs, phrases, and clauses. If you can't think of how something should be described, think of yourself as the reader and decide what you would want to know. Depending on what it is you're talking about, the reader might like to know:

• What size is it?
• How many are there?
• What is it made of?
• Where is it located?
• What is its condition?
• What is its use?
• Where did it come from?
• What is its value?
• What does it look/taste/smell/sound/feel like?

Naming and detailing call on the power of observation, but comparing calls on the power of imagination. Usually when you compare something, you will use either a **metaphor** or **simile.**

A metaphor compares two things that are not alike, but describes one as though it were the other: In Thomas Woolf's novel *Look Homeward, Angel,* he describes the North Carolina hills where his character grew up as a "bleak bare prison," then he presents the character looking back over the mountains at his home town of Altamont, and writes, "Altamont lay gray and withered in the hills, a bleak, mean, wintry dot." Both are effective metaphors: by saying the hills are a prison, he implies that they are something from which he wanted to escape. By saying the town is a bleak, mean dot, he expresses his feeling that his home town is

90

depressingly insignificant, and also suggests he never found much affection there.

A simile directly compares two things using the words *like* or *as*. Here is a passage from Norman McLean's novel *A River Runs Through It*. In this passage Norman is talking about his brother, Paul: "He came charging up the bank showering molecules of water and images of himself . . . and dripped all over us, like a young duck dog that in its joy forgets to shake itself before getting close. . . . At the end of this day, then, I remember him both as a distant abstraction in artistry and as a closeup in water and laughter."

This is beautiful description: "showering molecules of water and images of himself" is vivid and perfectly true, for each drop of water would have reflected Paul's image. There are two similes in the passage: "like a young duck dog that in its joy forgets to shake itself before getting close"--a very effective image--and "as a closeup in water and laughter." The first simile uses *like*, the second uses *as*.

You hear similes all the time--and that can be a problem. The whole purpose of using metaphors and similes is to enhance description by writing about something in a surprising new way that is suggestive and revealing. If you use a simile that has been used over and over, then you're using something predictable that has lost its power to be suggestive or reveal anything new. These are called *clichés*. Avoid them. Clichés such as "fast as greased lightning" or "raining cats and dogs" no doubt brought a smile to the first persons to hear them, and that is no doubt why they became clichés: they were so good that people kept repeating them. But now when we hear those expressions, we don't even think about being as fast as lightning that's been lubricated or raindrops as big as family pets. They don't register in our brains because they have been so overused that we don't even stop to visualize them.

Something else you want to do to make your scenes and people vivid is provide sensory details. Too often when we start describing scenes or characters, we rely only on the sense of sight; we write what things look like and leave it at that. But to create a vivid scene, you need to remember your other senses, as well.

Hearing--What do things sound like? You might mention the squeaking of a hinge, or the sputter of an engine.

Touch--You can use words like tingle, itch, and sting to describe how things feel, and you can also describe temperatures--hot, warm, cold, arctic--and textures--smooth, gritty, silky, soft, sticky.

Taste--Generally, of course, you will only describe taste when you've put something in your mouth. Words like bitter, sour, sweet, salty, spicy, sugary, and savory are useful.

Smell--Describing smells, or simply calling them to mind, can be especially effective. Here is another example from *A River Runs Through It* in which Paul and Norman are having a conversation when Paul brings up their high school locker room. Norman recalls, "I went on thinking until I noted that I could smell witch hazel, rubbing alcohol, hot radiators with sweat clothes drying on them, and the insides of boy's lockers that wouldn't be cleaned out until the end of the football season."

You see in that passage that he names things: witch hazel, rubbing alcohol, radiators, lockers. Then he adds descriptions through adjectives and clauses: hot radiators with sweat clothes drying on them, boys' lockers that wouldn't be cleaned out until the end of the football season. But the whole thing is tied together through the sense of smell. He is smelling each of the things he mentions.

An Indication of Significance

Personal narratives need a well-told story with vivid details. It also needs to have a point. Remember again that it is almost always better to show than tell. The meaning, the significance of your essay should be implied throughout. As you dramatize the events in your story, as the reader sees important scenes and people from your point of view, the reader will naturally identify with you. This identification allows the reader to feel the importance of the event. You should not have to end your essay with an explanation of why the event you've just written about is important. You may indicate how you felt at the time or how you feel now, and you can interpret the events. But the significance of the story should be clear from reading it. You shouldn't have to tag it on at the end, and you should avoid sounding as if you're moralizing or preaching.

Here is another passage from Thomas Woolf's "The Lost Boy." This passage occurs near the end of the book, with Eugene as an adult remembering his brother Grover, who had died during their childhood:

> The years dropped off like fallen leaves: the face came back again-- the soft dark oval, the dark eyes, the soft brown berry on the neck, the raven hair, all bending   down, approaching. . . . And he knew that he would never come again, and that lost magic would not come again. Lost now was all of it . . . absence in the afternoon, and the house that waited, and the child that dreamed. And out of the enchanted wood, that thicket of man's memory, Eugene knew that the dark eye and the quiet face of his friend and brother--poor child, life's stranger, and life's exile, lost like all of us, a cipher in blind mazes, long ago--the lost boy was gone forever, and would not return.

In this passage you can find a well-told flashback, good use of pacing, tension, vivid language including the simile "years dropped off like fallen leaves" and the metaphors "the enchanted wood, that thicket of man's memory" and "a cipher in blind mazes," and, of course, significance.

92

Brainstorming Activities for Personal Narratives

On a separate sheet of paper:
1. List people currently in your life who have an influence on you.
2. List people important to your life when you were in high school.
3. List people important to your life when you were in junior high.
4. List people important to your life when you were a child.
5. For each person you listed, make a list of events you associate with that person. (Note: Be sure to list the bad times with the good, the failures with the successes. Sometime our best personal stories involve adversity.)
6. List other events that have happened to you recently.
7. List other events that happened to you in high school.
8. List other events that happened to you in junior high.
9. List other events that happened to you as a child.
10. Go through your entire list of events, and for each event, list objects associated with that event (clothing, cars, sporting equipment, whatever comes to mind).
11. Now describe each object you've listed.
12. Think about the significance of each event. Is the event likely to have significance for readers? Again, remember that sometimes our best personal stories come from our failures rather than our triumphs. Your readers cannot completely share your exhilaration of having won a regional championship (or whatever), but readers can certainly share your misery, your overcoming adversity, and, usually, your wildest and craziest moments.
13. Choose an event to write about.
14. Think about sequencing. Should you start at the beginning, or is it better to start somewhere in the middle or near the end, then add all the details using flashback?
15. Continue to concentrate on descriptive writing. Make sure all the people in your story are described in some manner. Remember to use as many sensory images as appropriate in your descriptions (sight, sound, smell, touch, taste).
16. Think of ways to create tension or suspense in your story -- something to make the reader want to keep reading.
17. Don't forget about dialogue. It is probably important that readers hear your characters talk at some point in the story. Each character should have his/her own voice.
18. Remember that the significance of the event you describe should be clear from reading the story. You should not tack on the meaning at the end.

What is Not Appropriate in Undergraduate Papers

It is important that students feel free to express themselves openly in college classes, both during class discussions on in writing assignments. Thus, a great degree of liberty is given to students in the area of creative expression in freshman composition courses. Topics and language that are not acceptable in other classes often are allowed here.

However, there are limits. While creative expression is of great importance, a supportive, positive classroom environment for all students is even more important. A typical college classroom is composed of students from many racial and ethnic backgrounds and is likely to contain students who are gay or bisexual, or who are devout in their religious beliefs, whether those beliefs be Catholic, Seventh Day Adventist, Mormon, Bahaâi, Iglegias Ni Cristo, Buddhist, or something else. It is important that every member of the class look forward to coming to class.

Therefore, papers that are likely to offend, intimidate, disgust, or nauseate others in the class are not acceptable. These include the following:

1. Papers that single out any student in the class for personal attack or ridicule.
2. Papers that are racist, sexist, or homophobic.
3. Papers that contain excessive profanity. Some profanity may be necessary at times in contemporary writing--particularly in dialogue during an argument—to appear realistic, but excessive profanity exhibits limited vocabulary and a lack of writing skills.
4. Papers that contain graphic sex. There are bound to be students in class who would be offended. You can write about sex and even write about sex sensuously if it is done with good taste. But draw the line at graphic descriptions of sexual activity that readers might consider pornographic.
5. Papers that contain excessive violence. The criteria here is whether the descriptions of violent acts appear gratuitous (that is, violence just for the sake of violence, or if it appears you are consciously attempting to disgust or sicken your readers).

Suggestions for Effective Peer Editing

1. Exchange papers with someone in your peer group (groups of four or five students usually work best).
2. Each student should use a different colored pen and PRINT his or her name at the bottom of the first page.
3. Make corrections and comments directly on the paper.
4. While it is nice to compliment your classmates on what they've done well, it is even nicer to make corrections and offer suggestions that will help the student improve his/her paper.
5. Think about the purpose and requirements of the assignment to help you make constructive criticism.
6. Do not change contractions to two words. Words like *don't* and *couldn't* are fine.
7. Do not change first person to third person. First person is expected in most freshman papers, especially personal narratives and opinion papers.
8. If you are unsure about a correction, ask your instructor.
9. If you come across another editor's correction that you dispute, do not mark through it, but write your own comment to the author stating that you disagree.

The following are suggestions and questions to consider when editing and discussing exercises and stories. Not every item will be appropriate for every exercise or story.

1. How well does the paper address the instructions and requirements for the exercise?
2. Discuss the writing in relation to the basic elements of fiction writing. Which elements are done well? Which need to be improved? How could the latter be improved? Discuss elements such as:
   descriptive writing
   narration
   characterization
   plot
   tone
   organization
   sentence structure
   paragraphing
   pace
   tension
   word choice

3. Is the chosen verb tense and point of view the most effective choice for this piece? Would the story be better told in present (or past) tense? First (or third) person?

4. Discuss the style. How would you describe the style? Is it appropriate for the story?

5. Is there an indication of significance? Why was this piece written (other than to fulfill the class requirements)? Is it intended to scare you? To make you think? To make you fantasize? To entertain you? Did it succeed? Why or why not? Can you point to specific passages or elements that worked well and/or did not work well? How could it be made more successful?

6. Is there an emotional core (depth of feeling)? How could the writer make the piece more profound?

7. How does this piece compare with other pieces you've seen by this student? Is the writer developing a unique voice? If so, can you describe it? Do you like it, or do you find it irritating, condescending, boring, or worse? (As this is a sensitive area, please make sure you do not directly insult the student. But do find a way to suggest improvements that will help make the writer's work more appealing to you.)

8. Discuss story potentialities (i.e., is this piece worth pursuing, and, if so, how might it be developed into a longer work).

Logical Fallacies

Logical fallacies are errors in thinking and writing that at first glance appear to make sense but are in fact a result of faulty logic. The most common types are listed below. Some are called by more than one term. Please keep in mind that memorizing the names of the fallacies is not important. Understanding the reasoning behind the fallacy is.

Logical fallacies fall under the category of critical thinking. Democracies require critical thinking in order to function efficiently. Citizens cannot always trust their leaders to tell them the truth or the whole truth. It is critical that during campaigns an informed electorate contains a majority of people who can see through the logical fallacies included in campaign speeches and advertisements. If politicians are able to fool the majority of the people the majority of the time, that is bad news for democracy indeed. This could explain why some politicians choose the attack "the educated elite." They know that people with a good education, who have studied logical fallacies, can see through their lies. They don't like that.

This is also the reason that citizens with Ph.D.'s are rarely chosen for jury duty. Either the prosecuting attorney or the defense attorney usually knows during jury selection that the facts favor the other side and he or she will have to rely on logical fallacies in order to win the case. That attorney is going to prefer to seat jurors who easily can be manipulated by logical fallacies.

Unfortunately, in the United States, most citizens are bombarded with logical fallacies on a daily basis. They may not be serving as a juror, and they may not be paying attention to political ads, but they are certainly being inundated with advertising for various products, and these too often rely on fallacies. The companies producing the ads have one objective: sell, sell, sell. They will use any tactic that works.

As future scholars, however, college students do have a commitment to objectivity and pursuit of truth. When students write papers, they must be sure their arguments are based on true logic, not on logical fallacies. This, then, is one of the most important lessons you will learn in college, for the ability to avoid fallacies absolutely will improve the grades you receive on papers, and the ability to ferret out fallacies in the world around you could potentially save you from being misled by an unscrupulous salesperson, save you from convicting someone who is not guilty or setting a guilty person free, and, ultimately, make the country you live in a better place.

Hasty Generalization—A conclusion based on too little evidence, suggesting a superficial investigation of an issue. One sometimes encounters this on the local news if the "reporter on the street" interviews two or three people then, if they all agree, says something to the effect that the people of that area seem to agree on the matter. One cannot draw that conclusion based on such a small sample size—especially since the three people being interviewed may very well have just come out of the same political meeting happening next door.

Oversimplification—Occurs when an argument obscures or denies the complexity of the issue. These are often found in the form of slogans: Guns don't kill people; people kill people. Pro-choice. Pro-life. Gun control and abortion are complex issues and cannot be reduced to mere slogans. Oversimplification can be found in longer statement, too, of course. Any time a complex issue is reduced in scope so that a sweeping generalization can be made, chances are the issue is being oversimplified.

Either/Or Reasoning—Suggests that only two choices exist when, in fact, there are more. In politics this argument often takes the form of "either you're with me or you're against me." An example most of the world remembers is when President George W. Bush, in trying to assemble an international coalition to invade Iraq, made a statement implying that if countries chose not to support the invasion of Iraq they supported terrorists . He went on to say, "There is no neutral ground – no neutral ground – in the fight between civilization and terror, because there is no neutral ground between good and evil, freedom and slavery, and life and death." This is a wonderful example of the fallacy of either/or reasoning. Obviously, it is possible to be partially good or partially evil, partially free or partially enslaved, or in a coma. Either/or reasoning tries to paint the world in black and white when we all know there are many shades of grey. Either/or reasoning also tries to argue that only two choices exist when in fact there are many more options that could be considered.

Begging the Question—Distorts a claim by including a secondary idea that requires proof, though no proof is given. It is also called circular reasoning. An example: "If prostitution wasn't immoral then it wouldn't be against the law." Why is it against the law? Because it's immoral. Why is it immoral? Because it's against the law?" One can see why it is called circular reasoning. It is called begging the question because in this case the example begs the question, "What about prostitution makes it immoral and makes it something we should make illegal?"

Non Sequitur—Occurs when one statement is not logically connected to another. The term is a Latin phrase meaning "it does not follow." These occur frequently in political ads. The ad might say something like, "John Smith is a father, a farmer, and a veteran who knows the value of hard work. John Smith is highly qualified to be your next Governor." Well, there are obviously some fathers out there who might be qualified to be a good governor, and the same can be said for farmers and veterans. There are also many fathers, farmers, and veterans out there who are not. It does not follow that having those attributes qualifies John Smith to be governor.

Bandwagon—Suggests that if a majority of people express a belief or take an action, everyone else should think or do the same. This is the bullying argument. It often implies that since the majority believes something, a person is dumb as hell if he or she doesn't believe it too. The fallacy in this thinking is obvious. Majorities can be wrong. There was a time in this country when the majority of Americans thought women should not have the right to vote. There was a time when the majority of people felt interracial marriage was immoral. The bandwagon fallacy is also used to make illogical proclamations. Example: "Justin Bieber won the People's Choice award for Best Male Vocalist two years in a row. He is obviously the greatest male vocalist alive today." Tell that to lovers of opera.

Red Herring—An irrelevant issue introduced into a discussion to draw attention from the central issue. This term has a wonderful origin. There was a time in Great Britain when, if a prisoner escaped, authorities would use bloodhounds to track him down. Prisoners discovered that if they drug a red herring (a type of fish popular in Britain) across the trail, when the dogs got to that point they would become hopelessly confused and wander off in sundry directions. Politicians frequently introduce red herrings into an argument when they are trapped. If they have no good answer to the question, they will bring up a totally unrelated (or only marginally related) point that they know is popular to divert their audience's attention away from the issue at hand and the fact that they have no reasonable answer for the actual question being asked.

Post Hoc—Assumes that because one thing follows another, the first thing caused the second. This is another fallacy found frequently in politics. Example: "Since my opponent took office, his policies have caused unemployment to rise 4% and the average wage to fall by 2%." Everything always follows something else. If I get up this morning and this afternoon there is an earthquake in China, it would be ridiculous to suggest that my getting out of bed caused the earthquake. I'm not that fat, and I don't live in China. Likewise, although it certainly is possible that a politician's policies caused a downturn in the economy, there are many other factors that also could be to blame. One would need to show a direct correlation to establish cause and effect. Just saying this happened, then this happened, so the first thing caused the second, and offering no proof, is a post hoc fallacy.

Ad Hominem—A personal attack on the opponent(s) rather than on the opposing argument. Politicians do this all the time by unfairly trying to label their opponent or attacking his or her personal attributes rather than their policies. Unfortunately, this tactic very often works.

Poisoning the Well—Attempts to shift attention from the merits of an argument to the source or origin of the argument. Once more, this is a favorite of politicians. If the President is unpopular and a Republican, a Democrat running in a state election will try to link his or her Republican opponent with the unpopular President. Republicans do the same. Sometimes politicians will even go so far as to try to link their opponent with unpopular figures in history: "This is the same policy Adolph Hitler adopted for Germany in 1934." Few today would argue that Hitler was good, but that doesn't mean that every policy he enacted was bad. The argument should be made against the actual policy, if, in fact, it is a bad policy. By poisoning the well, the politician tries to associate his opponent with the unpopular Hitler so that voters will not even consider the merits of the policy.

False Analogy—A comparison that is not based on relevant points of similarity. Example: "Students are like nails. You have to hit them on top of the head to get them to work." This is a silly—and hopefully false—analogy because a student and a nail are dissimilar. For analogies to work, the things being compared must be similar.

Slippery Slope—Occurs when the writer argues that taking one step will lead inevitably to a second, undesirable step. Examples: "If we legalize marijuana, soon everyone will be addicted to heroin." "If we legalize gay marriage, soon people will want to marry their dogs." This scare tactic is more effective than one would think. Politicians and preachers use it frequently to try to prevent change. It is true that actions have consequences, but insisting that a reasonable action will inevitably lead to a tragic result is a fallacy. One must offer some reasonable proof that such a thing might realistically happen. Obviously, one would have a hard time proving that society is on the path to marrying animals if for no other reason than that marriage requires mutual consent and animals are incapable of giving consent.

Circular Definition—A definition that includes the term being defined as part of the definition. Example: "Freedom is the state of being free." From that, we still don't know what being "free" means, do we?

Straw Man—Occurs when the writer directs the argument against a claim that nobody actually holds or that everyone agrees is weak in order to misrepresent the true opposing argument. This is another tactic of politicians, and it is one of the most despicable because it is by definition a lie. When a candidate tells an audience that his opponent believes something the opponent does not in fact believe, or wants to do something the opponent does not in fact want to do, or doesn't care about a segment of the population that the opponent does in fact care about, those are all examples of a straw man. Another example: When asked about a new, expensive missile system, a candidate says, "I support it and my opponent opposes it. He would leave America defenseless." Perhaps the opponent has done his homework and knows the proposed missile system is too costly or inefficient or not needed. Perhaps he thinks it is being proposed primarily to help certain politicians with weapons factories in their districts. If that is the case, making the statement that he doesn't care about America's defense is a straw man, and also a lie.

Failing to Accept the Burden of Proof—Occurs when the writer asserts a claim but provides no support for it. These last few are straightforward. If one makes a claim, one must provide evidence to support it. One cannot make a claim and expect everyone to assume it's true. One is not God.

Emotional Appeal—Occurs when the writer tries to excite or appeal only to the reader's emotions. Politicians will do this be appealing to their audience's patriotism or, in the worst cases, their audience's prejudices. Emotional appeals also include sob stories. A candidate might mention losing a child or his wife's battle with cancer—anything to induce sympathy (and votes).

Ethical Appeal—Occurs when the writer tries to convince readers to accept an argument on the basis of his/her moral credentials. One often sees this in commercials when "experts" are called in to testify for a product. Never mind that they're being paid by the advertiser. Just believe them. Not.

Appeal to Tradition—Occurs when the writer's grounds rest solely on the "goodness" of what was been done in the past. America once had a tradition of slavery. America once had a tradition that only men who owned property could vote. We all appreciate certain traditions, but not all traditions are equal, and sometimes they need to be changed.

Samples of MLA Citations

A book with one author:

Caesar, Adrian. *Taking it Like a Man: Suffering, Sexuality and the War Poets: Brooke, Sassoon, Owen, Graves.* Manchester: Manchester UP, 1993.

Eby, Cecil Degrotte. *The Road to Armageddon: The Martial Spirit in English Popular Literature, 1870-1914.* Durham: Duke UP, 1987.

A book with two authors:

Brattin, Joel J., and Bert G. Hornback. *Our Mutual Friend: An Annotated Bibliography.* New York: Garland, 1984.

Brooker, Jewel Spears, and Joseph Bentley. *Reading The Waste Land: Modernism and the Limits of Interpretation.* Amherst: U of Massachusetts P, 1990.

A book with no author listed:

Missouri Scenic Roadways. Hartford, CT: Balliard, 2000.

More than one book by the same author:

Brooke, Rupert. *The Letters of Rupert Brooke.* Ed. Geoffrey Keynes. New York: Harcourt, 1968.

---. *The Prose of Rupert Brooke.* Ed. Christopher Hassell. London: Sedgwick, 1956.

---. *Song of Love: The Letters of Rupert Brooke and Noel Olivier.* Ed. Pippa Harris. New York: Crown, 1991.

A book with an editor:

Diekhoff, John S., ed. *A Maske at Ludlow: Essays on Milton's Comus.* Cleveland: P of Case Western U, 1968.

Patrides, C.A., ed. *Milton's Lycidas: The Tradition and the Poem.* Columbia: U of Missouri P, 1983.

A book with an author and an editor:

Eliot, T.S. *The Waste Land: A Facsimile and Transcript of the Original Drafts Including the Annotations of Ezra Pound.* Ed. Valerie Eliot. New York: Harcourt, 1971.

Periodicals:

Brattin, Joel J. "Dickens' Creation of Bradley Headstone." *Dickens Studies Annual: Essays on Victorian Fiction.* Vol. 14. Ed. by Michael Timko, et. al. New York: AMS, 1985. 147-65.

Gallup, Donald. "The `Lost' Manuscripts of T. S. Eliot." *Times Literary Supplement* 7 Nov. 1968: 1238-40.

Anonymous articles:
"Global Warming Melting Antarctic Ice Cap: Trouble Ahead." *Kansas City Star*. 23   August 2000. A17.

An essay in a book in which author and editor are the same:
Trilling, Lionel. "The Dickens of Our Day." *A Gathering of Fugitives*. Boston: Beacon, 1956. 41-48.

An essay in a book or journal with an editor:
Reed, John R. "Confinement and Character in Dickens' Novels." *Dickens Studies Annual*. Vol 1. Ed. by Robert B. Partlow, Jr., et. al. Carbondale: Southern Illinois UP, 1970. 41-54.
Tracy, Robert. "Reading Dickens' Writing." *Dickens Studies Annual: Essays on Victorian Fiction*. Vol. 11. Ed. by Michael Timko, et. al. New York: AMS, 1983. 37-59.

Letters (individual):
Lucas-Lucas, St. John. Letter to Richard Halliburton. 16 March 1928. Richard Halliburton Papers. Princeton University Library.
Olivier, Noel. Letter to Richard Halliburton. 27 Sept. 1927. Richard Halliburton Papers. Princeton University Library.
---. Letter to Geoffrey Keynes. 30 Nov. 1955. Geoffrey Keynes Collection. Department of Manuscripts and University Archives. Cambridge University Library.

Letters (collected and published):
Eliot, T. S. The Letters of T. S. Eliot. Ed. Valerie Eliot. Vol. 1: 1898-1922. San Diego: Harcourt, 1988.

Reviews:
Spender, Stephen. "Hidden Passion of the Neglected Poet." Rev. of *A.E. Housman: The Scholar-Poet* by Richard Perceval Graves. *NOW!* 9 Nov. 1979: 94-95.
Whipple, Edwin Percy. *Charles Dickens: The Man and His Work*. 1912. Boston: Houghton, 1975.

An interview you conducted:
Marsh, Patricia. Personal interview. 16 Dec 2014.

Published interviews:
Amis, Kingsley. "Mimic and Moralist." *Interviews with Britain's Angry Young Men*. By Dale Salwak. San Bernardino: Borgo, 1984.

Films:
For the Bible Tells Me So. Dir. Daniel Karslake. First Run Features. 2007.

The Future of Food. Dir. Deborah Koons Garcia. Iron Weed. 2007.

Paragraph 175. Dir. Rob Epstein and Jeffrey Friedman. New Yorker Films. 2000.

Waco: Rules of Engagement. Dir. William Gazecki. Fifth Estate Productions. 1997.

Television or radio program:

"The Blessing Way." *The X-Files.* Fox. WXIA, Atlanta. 19 Jul. 1998. Television.

Sound recordings:

Brown, Ian. *My Way.* Polydor, 2009. CD.

Curve. *The Way of Curve.* Anxious Records, 2004. CD.

O'Connor, Sinead. *I'm Not Bossy. I'm the Boss.* Nettwork, 2014. CD.

Roxy Music. *Roxy Music Live.* Eagle Records, 2003. CD

An article on a website:

Warner, Maxwell. "Bloomberg Mulls Run." *Politico.* The New York Times Company. 10 January 2008. 12 January 2008. Website.

Works Cited Exercise

Instructions: In groups of three or four student, turn each of the following sources into a Works Cited page entry. Do each one together as a group beginning with the first (you do not need to alphabetize the list for this assignment). Do not divide up the list between you. Each person in your group should write down the entries.

1. A book. Author: John Frayn Turner. Title: *Splendor and Pain.* Published in: London. Publisher: Breeze Press. When: 1992.

2. A book. Author: Michael Holroyd. Title: *Augustus John: A Biography.* Published in London in 1974 by Heinemann.

3. An anonymous newspaper article titled "Mr. Rupert Brooke: The Poet and Sub-Lieutenant Killed by Sunstroke." The article appeared on page 10 of the April 26, 1915, edition of the *Westminster Gazette.*

4. An article titled "The Georgian Renaissance" by D. H. Lawrence on pages 10-14 of the March 1913 edition of the magazine *Rhythm.*

5. A book by Adrian Caesar and Paul Bowles titled *Taking it Like a Man: Suffering, Sexuality, and the War Poets.* Published in Manchester, England, by Manchester University Press in 1993.

6. A personal interview with Bienvenido Santos that took place in Wichita, Kansas, on July 23rd, 1960.

7. An article written by Michael Stanton titled "Put an End to Violence" that appeared on the *cnn.com* website on July 9th, 2003. The site was accessed on July 10th, 2003, and the web address was www.cnn.com/iraq/stanton.

John Smith

English 101

Dr. Michael Wilson

30 Oct 2015

Sample MLA Paper

Set up your paper for double spacing, use Times New Roman 12 point font, with a ragged right margin (not justified), and add a header. In Microsoft Works, you click on "header" under the "view" tab. Simply switch the alignment to right align, type in your last name, a space, then go to the "insert" tab and click on page number. The computer will then automatically insert the correct number for each page. The margins on your paper should be one inch on all sides. The header is one-half inch from the top, but you should not have to worry about that since it is the default setting in most cases.

Your paper should look like the above example, giving your name, the course and section number, your instructor's name, and the date in the format shown (day, month, and year, without commas). After the date, hit the enter key then center the title. Do not boldface, italicize, underline, or capitalize all letters in the title. Just center it and capitalize the first letter of each word (except for words like "a," "the," "but," "for," etc.--unless the word is the first word of the title, in which case it too is capitalized). After you type the title, hit the enter key again and return to left alignment. Do not put extra line spaces before or after the title.

Everything in MLA style is double spaced. You never single space and you never insert additional line spaces.

You must provide a source citation for all information in your paper that is not common knowledge or is not your own idea or opinion. You should paraphrase or summarize information from other sources, then provide a parenthetical citation after the information. If all the information in the paragraph is from the same source, simply put the citation at the end of the paragraph (Jones 47).

The above citation would refer readers to your Works Cited page, where they should find one entry alphabetized under Jones. If they choose to consult your source, they would be able to locate the information because you have provided them with the page number in the citation above and with the publication information in the Works Cited listing. If you continue to use the Jones source for the next information, you do not need to repeat the author's name in your next citation; you can simply provide the new page number in your citation (52). You also do not need to give the name of the author in your citation if the author is identified in the paragraph itself. Example: According to Aubrey Jones, it is less expensive to travel to Europe in winter (97). For sources that do not have page numbers, such as most web pages, you should repeat the citation information for clarity (Warner).

If all the information in a paragraph is from the same source and page numbers, simply wait until the end of the paragraph to put the citation. If the source is the same but the page numbers change, do it as in the paragraph above. If your paragraph contains information from several sources, provide the citation information after each source (Lyons 10). Remember not to put the word *page* or the letter *"p"* in your parenthetical citation (Smith 452). Simply put the author's last name, a space, and the page number (Talbert 91). Also remember that the citation goes before the period (Lyons 112).

You should only use direct quotation if a passage is said so well in the original that you want your readers to experience the beauty of the language, or if you need to quote directly to avoid bias or error, or if the original was said so succinctly that you would use many more words to paraphrase than were used in the original passage. Your paper should never be more than ten percent direct quotation. "When you do use direct quotation," Smith advises, "punctuate it correctly and put the end quotation mark at the end of the quotation, then put the citation, then the final period" (Smith 43-44). If the quotation were a question, you would put the question mark before the end quotation mark and you would still put a final period after your citation.

The most important thing to remember is that all information from an outside source absolutely must have a citation ("Global" 23). If you do not credit the source, you are committing plagiarism, which is a serious offense, punishable by death in states that allow it (25).

Your Work Cited page should be a separate page with the words

Works Cited appearing at the top. After the title, simply double space and begin your list of works cited in the paper. You cannot list a work as "cited" if in fact there is no citation in your paper for that work. Works should be listed alphabetically by author's last name. If no author is given for a work, that work will be alphabetized on your Works Cited page by the first word of the title (but if the first word is *a, an,* or *the*, alphabetize by the second word). Thus, your parenthetical citation will also have the first word of the title--in quotation marks if it is the title of an article and in italics if it is the title of a book (*Missouri* 387-94).

Websites can be a challenge to cite. As a general rule, if you are citing an article on a website begin with the name of the author of the article, last name first, if an author is provided. If the article has a title, provide that next using quotation marks. Third, list the name of the website in italics. If the website is associated with an institution, list that information next. Your next two items are dates in MLA style (day, month, year, without commas): first, the date the information appeared on the website (if provided), then the date you accessed the website. Finally, put the complete web address for the article, or at least enough of the address to make the article easy to find (Warner). Put a period after each item in the listing.

Also remember to indent second, third, and fourth lines of your Works Cited items. Only the first line should be flush with the left margin.

Works Cited

"Global Warming Melting Antarctic Ice Cap: Trouble Ahead." *Kansas City Star.* 23 August 2000. A17.

Jones, Aubrey. *Planning a Vacation*: Seeing the World on the Cheap. New York: Dutton, 1997.

Lyons, Gene. *Whatever Happened to Those Good Old Days?* Little Rock: Empire, 1999.

Missouri Scenic Roadways. Hartford, CT: Balliard, 2000.

Smith, Elliot. *You Can Do What You Want to Whenever You Want To.* Boston: Little Brown, 1991.

Warner, Maxwell. "Bloomberg Mulls Run." *Politico.* The New York Times Company. 10 January 2008. 12 January 2008. www.politico.com/opinion/politics/maxwell.10

Observation Essay Rating Scale

___ Complete, peer-edited, double-spaced rough draft
___ Not complete or not peer-edited or not double-spaced
___ No draft

___ Proper MLA format. Final copy has title, is left-aligned, has page numbers in the upper right hand corner, is in an easy-to read typeface. Printer quality is good.
___ Final copy fails to meet all these requirements.

___ Paper meets length requirement.
___ Paper is too short or too long.

___ Paper contains a dominant impression (thesis) and is organized in a sensible manner.
___ The thesis could use some clarification, or the paper needs better organization.

___ Vivid presentation. Paper reflects a careful observation and contains both a general description and attention to specific details. Good use of sensory details, including sounds and smells.
___ Presentation needs to be more vivid.
___ Presentation needs to be much more vivid.

___ Very few problems with grammar.
___ Some problems with grammar.
___ Many problems with grammar.

___ Very few problems with punctuation, paragraphing, capitalization, and spelling.
___ Some problems with the above.
___ Many problems with the above.

Remembering Events Essay Rating Scale

____ Final copy has title, is left-aligned, has page numbers in the upper right hand corner, and is in correct font. Good printer quality.
____ Final copy fails to meet these requirements.

____ Paper meets length requirement.
____ Paper is too short or too long.

____ Paper is clearly about a remembered event and shows originality.
____ Paper is not clearly about a remembered event and/or lacks originality.

____ Story is well-told, with good use of tension.
____ Story could be better told, making better use of tension.

____ Vivid presentation, making good use of sensory detail, naming, detailing, and comparing, and showing rather than just telling
____ Presentation should be more vivid.

____ Clear indication of significance
____ Significance needs to be enhanced
____ Very little indication of significance

____ Excellent use of vocabulary and descriptive language. Good word choice. Good variety of sentence patterns. Good organization.
____ Some problems with the above.
____ Many problems with the above.

____ Very few problems with grammar
____ Some problems with grammar
____ Many problems with grammar

____ Very few problems with punctuation, paragraphing, and capitalization. No spelling errors.
____ Some problems with the above, and/or one or two spelling errors.
____ Many problems with the above, and/or more than two spelling errors.

Remembering People Essay Rating Scale

____ Final copy has title, is left-aligned, has page numbers in the upper right hand corner, and is in correct font. Good printer quality.
____ Final copy fails to meet all these requirements.

____ Paper meets length requirement.
____ Paper is too short or too long.

____ Paper is clearly about a remembered person and shows originality.
____ Paper is not clearly about a remembered person and shows originality.

____ Paper contains a vivid portrait, including a physical description and dialogue.
____ Portrait could be more vivid and/or make better use of dialogue.

____ Paper contains detailed anecdotes and scenes. Sensory details are used well.
____ Anecdotes and scenes need more detail and/or better use of sensory details.

____ The significance of the remembered person is clear.
____ The significance needs to be enhanced.
____ There is little or no indication of significance.

____ Excellent use of vocabulary and descriptive language. Good word choice. Good variety of sentence patterns. Good organization.
____ Some problems with the above.
____ Many problems with the above.

____ Very few problems with grammar
____ Some problems with grammar
____ Many problems with grammar

____ Very few problems with punctuation, paragraphing, and capitalization. No spelling errors.
____ Some problems with the above, and/or one or two spelling errors.
____ Many problems with the above, and/or more than two spelling errors.

Profile Essay Rating Scale

____ Good interview questions and notes turned in.
____ Interview questions and notes not completely impressive or not turned in.

____ Final copy has title, is left-aligned, has page numbers in the upper right hand corner, is in an easy-to-read typeface. Printer quality is good.
____ Final copy fails to meet all these requirements.

____ Paper meets length requirement.
____ Paper is too short or too long.

____ Paper contains a controlling theme (thesis) and is organized in a sensible manner.
____ Controlling theme needs clarification and/or paper needs better organization.

____ Vivid presentation, including a physical description, descriptions of nonverbal behavior, and good use of direct quotation.
____ Presentation needs to be more vivid.
____ Presentation is not vivid.

____ Paper is written in an informative, entertaining pace. Paper exhibits good word choice, a variety of sentence patterns, and originality.
____ Problems with the above.

____ Very few problems with grammar.
____ Problems with grammar.
____ Many problems with grammar.

____ Very few problems with punctuation, paragraphing, capitalization, and spelling.
____ Problems with the above.
____ Many problems with the above.

Taking a Position Essay Rating Scale

___ Final copy has title, is left-aligned, has page numbers in the upper right hand corner, and is in an easy-to-read typeface. Printer quality is good.
___ Final copy fails to meet all these requirements.

___ Paper meets length requirement.
___ Paper is too short or too long.

___ Paper contains a well-defined, controversial issue and clearly indicates your position.
___ Issue is not well-defined and/or controversial, and/or position is ambiguous.

___ Paper contains reasonable tone.
___ Problems with tone (tone is arrogant, insulting, extreme, etc.)

___ Argument is convincing, logical, and well-supported.
___ Argument is not fully convincing or well-supported.

___ Major counterarguments are acknowledged and either accommodated or refuted.
___ Major counterarguments not acknowledged and/or accommodated or refuted.

___ Excellent use of vocabulary and descriptive language. Good word choice, variety of sentence patterns, and organization.
___ Problems with the above.

___ Very few problems with grammar
___ Some problems with grammar
___ Many problems with grammar

___ Very few problems with punctuation, paragraphing, and capitalization. No spelling errors.
___ Some problem, and/or one or two spelling errors.
___ Many problems, and/or more than two spelling errors.

Proposing Solutions Essay Rating Scale

____ Final copy has title, is left-aligned, has page numbers in the upper right hand corner, and is in an easy-to-read typeface. Printer quality is good.

____ Final copy fails to meet all these requirements.

____ Paper meets length requirement.

____ Paper is too short or too long.

____ Paper contains a well-defined problem and proposes a particular solution.

____ Problem is not well-defined and/or proposal is ambiguous.

____ Paper contains reasonable tone.

____ Problems with tone (tone is arrogant, insulting, extreme, etc.)

____ Reasons and evidence are given to show the argument is feasible and has a decent chance of solving the problem.

____ Argument needs more supporting reasons and evidence.

____ Argument is not fully convincing or may not be feasible.

____ Readers' reservations and objections are adequately addressed. Alternative solutions are considered and rejected.

____ Readers' reservations and objections are not anticipated and/or adequately addressed. Some important alternative solutions are not considered.

____ Excellent use of vocabulary and descriptive language. Good word choice. Good variety of sentence patterns. Good organization.

____ Problems with some of the above.

____ Very few problems with grammar

____ Some problems with grammar

____ Many problems with grammar

____ Very few problems with punctuation, paragraphing, and capitalization. No spelling errors.

____ Some problems with the above, and/or one or two spelling errors.

____ Many problems with the above, and/or more than two spelling errors.

Argument Essay Rating Scale

___ Final copy has title, is left-aligned, has page numbers in the upper right hand corner, and is in an easy-to-read typeface. Printer quality is good.
___ Final copy fails to meet all these requirements.

___ Paper contains a well-defined, controversial issue and clearly indicates your position.
___ Issue is not well-defined and/or controversial, and/or position is ambiguous.

___ Paper contains reasonable tone.
___ Problems with tone (tone is arrogant, insulting, extreme, etc.)

___ Argument is convincing, logical, and well-supported.
___ Argument is not fully convincing or well-supported.

___ Major counterarguments are acknowledged and either accommodated or refuted.
___ Major counterarguments not acknowledged and/or accommodated or refuted.

___ All information from outside sources is acknowledged with parenthetical citation.
___ Problems with above.

___ Citations and Works Cited page follow MLA style.
___ Problems with above.

___ Excellent use of vocabulary and descriptive language. Good word choice. Good variety of sentence patterns. Good organization.
___ Problems with the above.

___ Very few problems with grammar
___ Some problems with grammar
___ Many problems with grammar

___ Very few problems with punctuation, paragraphing, and capitalization. No spelling errors.
___ Some problems with the above, and/or one or two spelling errors.
___ Many problems with the above, and/or more than two spelling errors.

Classification and Division Essay Rating Scale

____ Final copy has title, is left-aligned, has page numbers in the upper right hand corner, and is in an easy-to-read typeface. Printer quality is good. MLA format.

____ Final copy fails to meet all these requirements.

____ Paper contains a classification or division with categories resulting from the same principle.

____ Paper is not classification or division or has categories resulting from differing principles.

____ Paper contains a thesis statement and logical organization.

____ Problems with one or more of the above.

____ Categories are all at the same level. All significant and relevant categories are discussed.

____ Organizational problems.

____ Paper shows originality and is interesting to read.

____ Paper lacks originality or should be more interesting.

____ Excellent use of vocabulary and descriptive language. Good word choice. Good variety of sentence patterns. Good transitions.

____ Problems with the above.

____ Very few problems with grammar.

____ Some problems with grammar

____ Many problems with grammar

____ Very few problems with punctuation, paragraphing, and capitalization. No spelling errors.

____ Some problems with the above, and/or one or two spelling errors.

____ Many problems with the above, and/or more than two spelling errors.

Comparison/Contrast Essay Rating Scale

____ Final copy has title, is left-aligned, has page numbers in the upper right hand corner, and is in an easy-to-read typeface. Printer quality is good. MLA format.
____ Final copy fails to meet all these requirements.

____ Paper meets length requirement.
____ Paper is too short or too long.

____ Paper contains a comparison/contrast with a basis for comparison.
____ Paper is not comparison/contrast or compares two things with no basis for comparison.

____ Paper contains a thesis statement and compares the same points for each subject.
____ Problems with one or more of the above.

____ Paper has appropriate structure: either a subject-by-subject or point-by-point comparison.
____ Organizational problems.

____ Paper shows originality and is interesting to read.
____ Paper lacks originality or should be more interesting.

____ Excellent use of vocabulary and descriptive language. Good word choice, variety of sentence patterns, and transitions.
____ Problems with the above.

____ Very few problems with grammar.
____ Some problems with grammar
____ Many problems with grammar

____ Very few problems with punctuation, paragraphing, and capitalization. No spelling errors.
____ Some problems, and/or one or two spelling errors.
____ Many problems, and/or more than two spelling errors.

Making Evaluations Essay Rating Scale

____ Final copy has title, is left-aligned, has page numbers in the upper right hand corner, and is in an easy-to-read typeface. Printer quality is good.

____ Final copy fails to meet all these requirements.

____ Paper meets length requirement.

____ Paper is too short or too long.

____ Paper contains a clearly-defined subject.

____ The subject of this evaluation could use some clarification.

____ Paper contains reasonable tone.

____ Problems with tone (tone is arrogant, insulting, extreme, etc.)

____ Paper contains a clear, balanced judgment.

____ Judgment is vague and/or somewhat biased.

____ Paper contains a convincing argument with reasons for evaluation supported by evidence. Readers' objections and questions are adequately addressed. Comparison/contrast is used appropriately.

____ Problems with one or more of the above.

____ Many problems with one or more of the above.

____ Excellent use of vocabulary and descriptive language. Good word choice. Good variety of sentence patterns. Good organization.

____ Problems with one or more of the above.

____ Very few problems with grammar

____ Some problems with grammar

____ Many problems with grammar

____ Very few problems with punctuation, paragraphing, and capitalization. No spelling errors.

____ Some problems with the above, and/or one or two spelling errors.

____ Many problems with the above, and/or more than two spelling errors.

Short MLA Paper Rating Scale

____ Proper MLA format in paper, citations, and Works Cited. Final copy has title, is left-aligned, has page numbers in the upper right hand corner, is in an easy-to-read typeface. Printer quality is good.

____ Final copy fails to meet all these requirements.

____ All information from outside sources is properly cited.

____ Citations missing.

____ Paper meets length requirement.

____ Paper is too short or too long.

____ Paper is well-written. Paper is informative and organized in a sensible manner around a controlling theme.entertaining pace. Paper contains good word choice and a variety of sentence patterns.

____ Problems with the above.

____ Very few problems with grammar.

____ Problems with grammar.

____ Very few problems with punctuation, paragraphing, capitalization, and spelling.

____ Problems with the above.

Rhetoric Paper Checklist and Cover Sheet

____ Paper is formatted in MLA style with header information in upper left corner, centered title, with everything double spaced (and **only** double spaced, including space between header and title and title and first paragraph).

____ Title reflects position or thesis of essay.

____ Margins are one inch on all sides.

____ Standard 12-point font (Times New Roman preferred).

____ Good printer quality; neat appearance.

____ Page numbers in upper right corner of every page after page one.

____ Direct quotation used appropriately, sparingly, using MLA format.

____ Long quotations properly indented; all quotations properly introduced.

____ Citations in proper MLA format.

____ Works Cited at end of paper in MLA format.

____ Essay meets length requirement.

____ All information from sources, including textbook, cited appropriately.

____ Every citation corresponds with an item on the Works Cited page.

____ Every Works Cited entry corresponds with at least one text citation.

____ First paragraph states thesis of essay from book and adequately summarizes the main arguments of the essay.

____ Your position is clearly indicated in thesis statement in second paragraph.

____ Argument is well-supported with logic. No logical fallacies.

____ Counter-arguments are considered and either refuted or accommodated.

____ Reasonable tone.

____ Essay is well-organized.

____ Grammatical mistakes do not frustrate readers' understanding.

____ Correct punctuation.

____ Correct spelling (use spell check!).

____ Appropriate word choice.

____ A variety of sentence structures demonstrating adequate writing skills.

Research Paper Checklist for MLA-Style Paper

1. Your paper is on the assigned topic or an acceptable topic and meets your instructor's guidelines.
2. Your heading and title are in MLA style.
3. Your title reflects the topic and position of your essay.
4. Margins are one inch on all sides.
5. Paper is in 12-point Times New Roman font.
6. Good printer quality; neat appearance.
7. Last name and page number in upper right corner of every page, MLA style.
8. Separate Works Cited page titled Works Cited.
9. Works Cited page alphabetized and in MLA format.
10. Essay meets length requirement.
11. Essay meets requirement for number of sources.*
12. Direct quotation used appropriately, sparingly, using MLA format.
13. Long quotations properly indented; all quotations properly introduced.
14. Citations in proper MLA format.
15. All information from sources, including textbook, cited appropriately.
16. Every citation corresponds with an item on the Works Cited page.
17. Every Works Cited entry corresponds with at least one text citation.
18. Paper does not over-rely on one source.
19. At least half of your sources appear to be objective.
20. At least half of your sources come from books or academic journals.
21. If an argument paper, you have a clear position indicated in thesis statement in first or second paragraph.
22. If an argument paper, argument is well-supported with logic. No logical fallacies.
23. If an argument paper, counter-arguments are considered and either refuted or accommodated.
24. You maintain a reasonable tone.
25. Essay is well-organized. Correct grammar. Correct punctuation. Correct spelling. Appropriate word choice. A variety of sentence structures. Sophisticated use of the English language.

   * Dictionaries, encyclopedias, and religious texts such as the Koran or the Bible are usually not considered when counting the number of sources. If you use one of these sources, simply identify the source within the paragraph. Parenthetical citations and Works Cited entries are not necessary for these sources.

Portfolio Checklist

Pros

___ Complete
___ Papers fulfill the elements of the assignments
___ Typed paper meets length requirement
___ In-class essays are of adequate length
___ Essays have gone through multiple revisions
___ Good use of descriptive writing
___ Good use of sequencing
___ Good grammar and punctuation

Cons

___ Incomplete
___ Papers do not fulfill the assignments
___ Papers do not meet length requirements
___ Papers have not been adequately revised
___ Writing needs to be more descriptive (see back pages of syllabus)
___ More attention needs to be paid to organization and sequencing (see back of syllabus)
___ Errors in grammar and punctuation are distracting or cause confusion
___ More time needs to be spent on the essays

Watersgreen House online:
http://watergreen.wix.com/watersgreenhouse

Visit us online at http://watergreen.wix.com/watersgreenhouse